M000207722

WHISPERS

FROM ANOTHER

ROOM

A Mystic's Journey into the World of Spirit

Joy Andreasen

Copyright © 2020 by Spirit Watch Enterprises.

All rights reserved. No part of this publication may be reproduced, distributed, or transmitted in any form or by any means, including photocopying, recording, or other electronic or mechanical methods, without the prior written permission of the publisher, except in the case of brief quotations embodied in reviews and certain other noncommercial uses permitted by copyright law.

Cover Design by 100Covers.com
Interior Design by FormattedBooks.com

ISBN 978-0-9898771-2-1 (Paperback)

PREFACE

"Having had the pleasure to know the author personally, I am at a distinct advantage in my enjoyment of this book as I can hear it in her voice and her inflection that adds to an already warm literary experience. I can tell you firsthand that Joy is as sweet as the droplets of honey that she leaves for the ants outside of her home. In "Whispers From Another Room", spirit communicator and shamanic energy healer Joy Andreasen, respectfully brings us her personal stories, soul healing experiences, and understandings of the spiritual realm as it has made itself known to her. These pages are filled with layers of ideas about our perception of time, energy, life, death, and ourselves. The reader is invited to explore the connections presented between the smallest blade of grass and each droplet of rain that falls; the energies that are present in our lives as they intersect and interact with those from those who came before. Joy's distinct and precise guidance will safely guide you through what she rightly calls an "ocean of awareness". My personal reminder to all of you is that we are spirits living in this material world. We are not from here, and nor do we stay here. This Earth, our island home, is just a temporary stay over for our souls as they explore and learn from this human experience. This world is busy, noisy, and overflowing with distractions. In reading this wonderful collection of ideas and thought-provoking experiences, one cannot help but to hear the call to be still, to slow down, and to listen to the whispers in their ear, to the songs in their heads, and to those that come to us from just beyond the curtain of the other side."

—Dustin J. Pari
Motivational speaker, Paranormal Investigator,
"Ghost Hunters" and "Ghost Hunters International"

CONTENTS

NOTE TO READERS

As I re-tell the stories of my visits with the other "rooms" of possibility, I will graciously and tactfully change the names of the subjects of my stories, unless they have given me permission to use their names. The cool thing is, you are not going to know whose names are real and whose are made up. As a precaution, I changed certain identifying details to protect my clients', family's, and friends' identities, as long as it does not change the point of the story. Occasionally I may mention someone famous who talked to me and in that case, they are who I say they are. They don't come around talking all that often so when they do, I am going to talk about it!

Some of the stories in this book may be repeated or appear in another book I have written. I tend to repeat myself sometimes. It drives my husband crazy but that is just the way it is.

THE OTHER ROOM IN THE SPIRIT WORLD

(My favorite poem about death, passed along to me when my dad died. By Henry Scott Holland.)

> "Death is nothing at all.
> It does not count.
> I have only slipped away into the next room.
> Nothing has happened.
> Everything remains exactly as it was.
> I am I, and you are you, and the old life that we lived so fondly
> together is untouched, unchanged.
> Whatever we were to each other, that we are still.
> Call me by the old familiar name.
> Speak of me in the easy way which you always used.
> Put no difference into your tone.
> Wear no forced air of solemnity or sorrow.
> Laugh as we always laughed at the little jokes
> that we enjoyed together.

Play, smile, think of me, pray for me.
Let my name be ever the household word that it always was.
Let it be spoken without an effort,
without the ghost of a shadow upon it.
Life means all that it ever meant.
It is the same as it ever was.
There is absolute and unbroken continuity.
What is this death but a negligible accident?
Why should I be out of mind because I am out of sight?
I am but waiting for you, for an interval,
somewhere very near, just round the corner.
All is well.
Nothing is hurt; nothing is lost.
One brief moment and all will be as it was before.
How we shall laugh at the trouble of
parting when we meet again! 🙰

Early one Sunday morning, my husband and I were just starting our day. We had my grandson over for the weekend and we were getting ready to prepare his breakfast. Just another normal morning, or so we thought.

From another room, we heard my mother's voice call out, "Hayden."

All three of us heard her voice. My husband and I both recognized the voice as my mother's. Nothing out of the ordinary you say? But my mother had died when Hayden was less than a year old and he was now four.

From time to time something happens. We are going about our business living life, eating breakfast, driving to work, or laying our heads down to sleep, and there comes a whisper, a sound, a soft breeze, or perhaps the lines of an obscure song whistling about in our thoughts.

It's almost as if the sound is a whisper from another room.

Many times, we ignore it. We turn on the radio to drown out the tune in our heads. We quickly dismiss the familiar voice of our mothers, the sound of a baby crying, or the almost indiscernible caress of an invisible hand as it touches our hair.

I'm Movin' On

When my mother passed, I drove, with my daughter, sixteen hours from my house to my mother's with the noise of my daughter's favorite country music group droning over and over to help pass the time.

At some point, one of the songs caught my attention.

Despite the fact that my mother had no interest or knowledge of country music, I am fairly sure she was telling me goodbye in the words of the song that I listened to over and over on the quiet nighttime drive to where her lifeless body lay awaiting our arrival to say our goodbyes.

About a month before her death, I had telepathically communicated with her and told her it was okay to move on. We would be okay without her. She had painfully held on for years past what was expected for those with her type of cancer. The song? "I'm Movin' On."

Interestingly enough, my dad did the same thing nine years later. He had not passed yet, but I found myself making the drive once again to Florida, this time all alone. A song began to play that talked about seeing the light and I knew his days were numbered. He passed less than two weeks later. Strangely enough, this particular song was a popular one at that time. I had heard the song many times on the radio, and had received no such message. It wasn't until this day at this moment that the song meant exactly what it meant.

As a Spirit communicator and shamanic energy healer, I have a room in my home affectionately named my healing room. It contains all of my tools of the trade: feathers, stones, candles, books, and divination cards. It is in this room where seekers sometimes come to talk to their loved ones on the other side (or other room), where I delve into the Spirit world to gain wisdom and information from my benevolent helpers, and where I often go to talk to Spirit.

There are many worlds, or rooms, other than the ones we live in.

Life is not just waking up, going to work, coming home, and going to bed. All of the moments that happen in between the normal everyday humdrum of existence are what make our hearts beat, the sun shine, and the moon glow. Many times, we are too busy to pay attention.

I think one of the main messages that our loved ones on the other side want to get across to us is to be happy. Sometimes we may feel guilty feeling joy when we are living our lives without the person we love. We think that we should be sad, or not enjoy life completely without them. If they truly love us, they want us to know that their passing was not a sad thing. They are just in another room, watching, loving, and waiting until the day we join them.

What follows is my musings of what happened when I began to pay attention to the whispers in the other room.

CHAPTER ONE

GHOST HUNTING:
WHO IS HUNTING WHO?

I remember when my second husband decided to take up "ghost hunting"—a term he hates, by the way; he prefers "spirit investigation." When he first started, he was inspired by a popular television reality show, so I use this term affectionately. I was horrified, however. It was my perception that living humans were using spirits as entertainment. At that point I had not disclosed to him that I could perceive spirits or that they communicated with me. I had stuffed the gift down and decided that since I was not in an environment where the gift had benefited me or anyone else, I was not going to use it or even acknowledge it.

Born Pentecostal, there was a small area of acceptance of the world of Spirit. That spirit was the Holy Spirit and He was the only one we listened to. If a voice other than the Holy Spirit or Jesus Himself came to us, that voice was deemed to be the voice of the devil or one of his cohorts. I do have childhood memories of experiences that could be considered out of the ordinary. However, over time, the ability to see or sense Spirit was silenced.

Years later I happened upon a community of Christians who communicated with the voice of the (Holy) Spirit and messages from that voice were readily accepted, given and received. At that moment I finally felt validated and believed I had found my home. My gifts were finally recognized and nurtured. My best friend was the resident "prophet." I was soon receiving and giving messages and I knew I had found my purpose. For a while.

Eventually Spirit got a little bold and unconventional with me and started telling me things that were not really accepted or understood in that environment. I left the church confused, disillusioned, and a bit disgruntled. I eventually divorced my first husband, stopped listening to the voices, and was determined to start a new existence away from the voice of Spirit. Enter second husband, Clay.

Sure, we had obstacles to overcome with blended family and the tensions that come from divorce, re-marriage, his children, my child, health concerns, and attempting to make all that work. But my focus had shifted away from receiving messages and more toward evolving myself spiritually and just plain enjoying my life. I had a mate who had a healthy curiosity for different spiritual beliefs as I did but no active interest in anything specific. I do remember telling him while we were dating that if he got "born again" all deals were off, but that is another story.

....Somebody's Ringin' the Bell

Then Clay's brother, Ray, died.

Ray's spirit began visiting the house on occasion. I was vaguely aware of his presence and would sometimes refer to him, jokingly, when odd things would happen in the house. Ray liked to ring the doorbell. My husband dismissed with disdain my wanting to open the door to let Ray in. He was the voice of reason to my insistence that almost everything is a sign. However, secretly, he desired communication with that other "room" where his brother, and other loved ones, resided.

In order to come to terms with his grief, Clay developed an interest in researching life after death and what is known as paranormal investigating, or ghost hunting. I was not terribly fond of his new obsession, but I comforted myself in the thought that it was a phase and he would grow bored with it over time. He didn't.

On the one hand, I think my Pentecostal upbringing made me a little nervous about the spirit investigations. What if Clay brought home a spirit? I also felt like he was really not doing anything to help the souls that he was attempting to contact. I used to accuse him of using ghosts for entertainment, not understanding that he was just exploring the idea of intelligent, conscious souls that did not inhabit a physical body. I did not understand that perhaps some of the souls did not necessarily need any help but wanted to communicate. Maybe they were actually hunting us! So, for the most part, Clay explored this new fascination with non-physical entities without me.

> Who is hunting who? Spirit would not leave me alone! I had left the church, stopped listening to or receiving Spirit messages, divorced my husband, remarried what I thought was a healthy skeptic, and this happens!!

Eventually Clay was successful in dragging me along to various paranormal events. My gift began to re-emerge as I surrendered my reluctance to use my gifts. Clay had never witnessed me using my gifts, and I had never spoken of it, so he was a bit surprised when I confessed, I could communicate with the dead and other benevolent helpers not in human form. Eventually he got used to the idea that he was married to a medium, and now he is my biggest supporter.

I believe that there is communication happening all the time, but we are rarely open to receiving it. We quickly dismiss anything out of the ordinary. If we hear sounds in the house, we dismiss them as the house settling, or perhaps a stray breeze blowing through and causing doors to close. The songs in our heads are just arbitrary and the flowery scents of our grandmothers' perfumes do not mean they are in the next room, just "dying" to catch our attention.

Over the years I have re-opened myself to the gift of conversing with Spirit. By relaying the messages they give me, I have been instrumental in bringing peace and healing not only to people, but animals, and even places that carried the emotions of pain and trauma left by events that happened in that location.

All the while I maintained my job at the post office, and tried to live a somewhat quiet and normal life as wife, mother, and grandmother.

CHAPTER TWO

RESPECT FOR
NON-PHYSICAL ENERGY

Most people who are interested in exploring the paranormal have watched at least one of those television shows where spirit investigators go into so-called haunted locations to have experiences and recount them to their viewers. They may also be hoping to receive audible or visible evidence of the existence of something or someone not in physical form. In many of these shows, the investigators engage in shouting, threatening, or otherwise challenging the "ghosts" to do something like scratch them, pull their hair, or some other outlandish actions that would probably boost the show's ratings. I find this practice disgusting and disrespectful to those who lack a physical body. Would you challenge someone to do those things if they were standing in front of you? (Well, maybe you would if you were in one of those ridiculous but insanely popular reality shows, but at least in those cases, everyone is there by choice!)

Admittedly, if the investigators are in a prison or mental health facility, the energy that resides there is probably not full of cotton candy and cupcakes. Despite the character traits of the person when they were alive, there is no reason to challenge them to continue in this behavior now that they are separate from their bodies. I would hope that if a soul is not at rest and I, or another spirit investigator run into them in a physical location, our desire would be to help them obtain peace or go to the light. When I finally began to accompany my husband on spirit investigations, it was with the sole intention of tuning in to the energy and helping in some way. Remember that energy is attracted to like energy, so if an investigator is shouting, threatening, or challenging a spirit, they are more likely to attract a not-so-nice entity. This is disrespectful and unethical.

We also have to remember that it is not only the souls of the deceased that have intelligence and consciousness. It is the belief of the earth-based systems, such as shamanism, that *everything* has consciousness and some form of intelligence. Science is beginning to confirm this through many experiments in quantum physics. There have been experiments with plants and water that prove the effects of our thoughts and intentions on items that have long been thought dead or lifeless such as rocks, chairs, feathers, land, or even our computers!

Ask Permission First!

When I first learned the art of crossing over earthbound souls, I enjoyed going out and finding them in various locations. One time my husband and I were out exploring and happened upon a tunnel that made its way through the middle of a mountain. In the middle of the tunnel, if you did not have a flashlight, it was completely dark. There was a waterway and a walking path that went through the tunnel and was part of a hiking trail in West Virginia. When we got to the middle of the tunnel, we turned off our flashlights and I began to tune in. I felt a great deal of energy in the tunnel and successfully crossed over a number of souls.

Surprisingly, I connected with a consciousness that introduced itself as the spirit of the tunnel. He told me that he was the guardian of the tunnel and had been so since its inception. I then asked if it was okay with him to be doing the work that I was doing, and I received this reply: "I would have liked for you to ask permission first." At that moment I was made aware of the aliveness of every location. Each blade of grass, each stone, each drop of water, carries with it its own intelligence and its own preferences and insights. If we are going to do this work, it should be with the guidance and assistance of the helping spirits that are all around us.

Just cus it's not from the "Light" doesn't mean it's "bad"

I was at a shamanic event in a remote location in Pennsylvania which was dedicated to earth-based religion. I was waiting my turn to enter a sweat lodge. This is a ritual that produces spiritual cleansing and experiences through the use of heat coming from what are called "stone people." These are heated through fire and placed inside a small tent or covered area.

As I stood in the natural setting, I immediately felt the presence of a large red bird beside me. This was not a natural bird, like a cardinal but a Spirit Bird, as large as a person. Using my extensive training in spirit communication, I asked if the presence was from the Light. I heard the immediate reply, "What if I am not? Not everything that is not from the Light is necessarily bad." This was an 'aha' moment for me. I had never considered that there were spirits of the earth and that they could be benevolent.

I immediately became aware of what earth-based people had already known. The earth is alive and intelligent. Each manifestation of intelligence, whether it is water, air, earth, or fire, has within it intelligence and wisdom. We would be wise to respect that consciousness and ask for its blessing as we go about our lives.

Now, before picking up a stone or picking a flower, or even buying plants at the nursery, I ask them for their permission to be a part of my life, whether it be to engage in a ritual or to be used for healing purposes. I have taught my grandchildren and my students that each tool they use in their spiritual practice, each morsel of dirt, feather, or stone, needs to grant permission before being used or taken from its location. It is also important to give a gift back when taking something from nature. I will offer gifts to the critters with whom I share my living space. I often give the ants gifts of water or honey or something sweet. Even flies and mosquitoes deserve respect and gifts of peace.

Gifts of Peace

The other day I was working at my desk and was being harassed by a fly that insisted upon buzzing around my head and alighting on various parts of my skin. At first, I was shooing him away, cursing under my breath, and swatting at his skilled navigation around my clumsy attempts to remove him from his life force. I could almost hear him giggling with glee as I chased him all around my desk. Sometimes I think the sole purpose of flies is to annoy us and when they succeed, they feel like they are accomplishing their mission in life. However, I also believe that our emotions play a huge part in the interaction. The more perturbed we become, the worse the interaction.

Remembering that I had some dried fruit stashed away in the bottom drawer of my filing cabinet, I formulated a truce. I took a couple pieces of dried fruit and offered them to him in trade for leaving me alone. I cunningly placed the morsels of sugarcoated pineapple and mango about ten feet away from my desk in an obscure section of a large filing cabinet behind me. Mr. Fly immediately ceased his relentless game with my sanity and we became fast friends.

It is now my practice to give peace offerings to all the little critters with whom I share space on the planet. Gifts of honey and fruit keep ants out of my home (most of the time—they do have free will too, you know!) I imagine that a little bit of blood may keep the mosquitoes away although I have not yet tried it. When I retrieve an item like a stone or a feather or even a stick to be used in ritual or in a fire pit, I offer a gift back to nature for its service. If I don't have a gift with me, I will break off a piece of my hair and present it to the earth with thanksgiving for its offering to me.

As an aside note, I recently decided to engage in a mostly plant-based diet and one of the immediate side effects I noticed was that mosquitoes no longer find me enticing! In years past it seemed I could not walk out of the house without being targeted! I now find only the occasional bite!

I have not been able to verify that this has been true of other plant-based eaters but it seems to have happened to me! Sometimes I wonder if the creatures of the earth are saying "thank you for not eating us."

Remember that there is so much more than our own little world we live in. This earth we live on has been here much longer than we have and will continue on in some form after we have gone. Respect for the non-physical energy is paramount to having a lifetime of cooperation and peace with our neighbors—the plants and creatures of the earth.

CHAPTER THREE

RELEASING TRAPPED EMOTIONS

As I mentioned before, I did not accompany Clay on his spirit investigations when he first began doing that. He wanted me to go along and he did invite me, but I was not interested in spending the night in haunted locations, sitting in the dark with various tools Clay and his team used to detect spirit activity, and then spending hours listening to recordings and watching video that had been obtained during the investigation. Don't misunderstand me; this is an important part of a spirit investigation. Obtaining evidence is crucial in proving out-of-the-ordinary occurrences. It just did not interest me. I like to sleep at night. I could detect Spirit without the gadgets. Sometimes the gadgets will pick up information which coincides with the information I am given and sometimes not so much.

Nowadays, however, Clay will often take me on the initial walk-through, which normally happens during the day. It is easy for me to sense energy, and often I am greeted by the resident spirit or another intelligent energy when I arrive. I must explain that not every knock, rap, footstep, or creak in the floor is paranormal. There is a normal settling of houses and often there is an imprint in the location, usually an emotion that represents someone's experience there. It is an old shamanic belief that is not very well understood in our modern consciousness, that everything has its own intelligence. Emotions are no exception. Emotions are what drive our earthly experience. Strong emotions often leave residue in the locations where they occur.

Many times, what people sense as ghosts are really just the strong emotions that individuals left in a location. Sometimes the emotions were so strong that a piece of someone's energy, possibly their soul, was left there and remains in the location. That piece of energy stays there, until someone like me becomes aware of it and is able to heal the emotion and release the energy either back to the individual who may or may not be dead, or help the energy go to the light. I never return the energy back to the individual without first leading it to a place of healing. This is usually accomplished by surrounding it with light and the Love of the Divine. I am always tuning in to my Guides for instructions on each individual emotion. Each of us as a soul is unique and, therefore, healings are also unique.

Sometimes I tune in to the event that caused the strong emotion and help the emotion, or stuck piece of soul, realize that the event has long since been over, and it is okay to move on. I will call upon others who the soul may be connected to and show them that time has passed and it is okay to heal and let it go. If it is resistant, I call upon the help of the Light—some call Angels—to bring about a healing or to transfer it to the Light for a reprogramming.

The Room of Grief

One of the first times Clay took me along on an initial contact with a client, I encountered a soul piece in one of the bedrooms of the house. She was blond with a ponytail, and I saw she was crying. I did not believe she was a ghost or that she was even dead. I believed she was a previous resident of the house. She was alive somewhere and was living out her life, but she had experienced something which had caused her a great deal of grief and had expressed that grief in this room. The current resident of the house had confided in Clay that she would experience great sadness in this room. Clay had not told me any of the claims of the residents, which is his policy, so that the information I might receive will not be tainted by their stories.

This was early on in our collaborations with spirit investigation and I was not comfortable yet sharing the information I received. I believed then, and still believe, in honoring the spirits and souls with confidentiality. I did not share with Clay what I saw during that investigation. As I am not bound with time or space when doing a healing, I went home, went out in our backyard, and connected with this soul piece distantly. With her permission that I had received telepathically, I led her in a healing and reconnected her soul piece with her soul living out her life somewhere else.

Since I had not shared with Clay what I had done, initially he and his team went back to the location, set up their equipment, and spent the night in the location. After hours of reviewing evidence, they had nothing to report.

Clay was a little frustrated, to say the least. I finally confessed that I had healed the soul of the girl in the bedroom, and sent her soul piece to her over-soul still living in another location. Clay was happy that I had healed her but suggested that I tell him next time so that he and his team wouldn't spend hours trying to detect energy that was no longer there.

Apparently, the resident of the house ceased experiencing sadness in that room and all turned out well.

Crying Babies and their Mommas

Another time, Clay took me and my mentor, Susan Lynne, a well-established psychic medium, to a location where the resident of the house would experience, among other things, the sound of a baby crying. As is his custom, Clay did not tell Susan or me that information.

As soon as I arrived, I saw a woman crying and felt the loss of a baby or small child. When I went into the house, I was able to pinpoint the room where she would sit and cry, or perhaps even hold the child and rock her before her death. I opened the window in the room and released her grieving soul to the light, where the soul of the lost child greeted her.

The room turned out to be where the current resident of the house would hear a small child crying. Not coincidentally, the current resident had lost more than one child at or about the age of three. My mentor, Susan, received the information that she was the reincarnation of the first woman who lived there. Due to the unresolved grief in that past life, she had re-experienced the same event in this life. We were able to help that part of her soul find resolution so that she would not reincarnate again and suffer the same experience in her next life. Obviously, the reincarnation is not verifiable, but it is interesting that she had chosen that house to call her home and that she had experienced the same event we had picked up on.

One of the members of Clay's team was proficient in checking census records and was able to verify that indeed, a woman lost a three-year-old child in that house in the distant past.

It is often fun and beneficial to go to locations with other mediums. We are all a bit different in our styles of receiving information. We may receive the same information or we may receive different information. It is like piecing together a jigsaw puzzle. Time rests in locations in layers, much like the layers of the earth. Time is not necessarily linear. We are able to detect layers of energy and existence in particular locations. One of us may detect one period of time, and another of us will detect another. It gives a picture of the history of the location perhaps even before the house or other structure was built.

The wild card, however, is the little understood fact that there is no time and space in the non-physical world. Many who like to go to historical locations hoping to connect with the historical figures that lived or experienced tragedies in the location are not necessarily the spirits that they run into while investigating.

You have to remember that we all walk around in this world emitting a frequency that is like a radio signal to the spirit world. If you are mean, angry, sick, depressed, or use a lot of mind-altering substances, you are going to attract a different energy than if you are mostly happy, content, and well balanced. That is why on television some of the paranormal stars get scratched, bitten, and all of those yucky experiences. These occurrences are a result of their insults, screams, and challenges that they make to the spirits themselves. It hurts my heart when I see this.

Sometimes it is hard for me to connect with certain people who have died in drug overdoses, suicides, and other traumatic events due to the fact that their energy is not compatible with mine. I have to set aside my own energy and blend with theirs in order to connect with them. It is almost like stepping into their consciousness. If I go to a location without any idea of what has occurred, and the soul is recently departed and in a low vibratory state, I may have trouble at first connecting with their energy.

I'm Sorry

On one recent occasion, a family called Clay and I to a house they were selling after having owned it for less than a year. They did not tell me any details, hoping I would be able to decipher what had happened in the house. I walked through the house and was able to describe the energy in each room: a young woman hunched down in the corner of one of the rooms, another room was occupied by a promiscuous male, a room where I heard music playing, and other incidentals. But what the family was really looking for was for me to connect with their son who had committed suicide in the room where I heard music. It had taken months for the father to clean up all the blood from the event, but I did not initially pick up on any of that. The young woman I had seen in one of the rooms was actually someone who had been there when this family bought the house, still alive somewhere. The way I described her was what the mother had seen when she walked through the house before she purchased it. She also confirmed the room where I sensed a lot of sexual activity when she explained that her son's roommate often had various and frequent female visitors.

I am not sure how much information she actually shared with me before I was able to connect with her son, but holding a necklace that he had made for her eventually brought him into awareness. I was disappointed in myself for not picking up on her son at first, but I did sense his shame and remorse over the event. Perhaps he was still in that in-between place where many souls of suicide end up until they have had some time to heal from whatever caused the despair precipitating the event in the first place. Interestingly enough, on my husband's recorder was a voice whispering, *raise your energy.* The voice seemed male. Was it the voice of my Guide telling me to raise my energy or was the son suggesting I raise my energy so I could sense him?

After holding the necklace, I was able to connect with him. I think he was hesitant to talk due to his shame, but the session seemed to be healing for both mother and son. Later we received an email from the mother saying that the session had indeed helped her process her grief.

In this particular case, the emotions were not initially evident to me in the room where the event had occurred, indicating that the suicide may have happened when he was not in his purely conscious mind. Drugs often affect a person's ability to discern the gravity of their actions. For me, it is sometimes difficult to connect with souls who left this earth while on drugs. I can almost feel their foggy state of mind. As I blend with their energy, I feel confused and it is sometimes difficult to convey any helpful information. This normally occurs when the death is fairly recent. After their soul has had time to be on the other side for a period of time, connecting to them is often much easier. A few months later one of the boy's friends came for a reading and I was able to connect with him fairly easily. I think by that time he had been on the other side long enough to have settled in and he was thinking much more clearly.

Remember that emotions carry their own energy, and sometimes when you experience a powerful emotion, that emotion remains in the location of the event that caused it. At times a part of your own essence or soul may remain with the emotion. Sometimes it remains with a person of significance or gets caught in the time period where the emotional event took place. This is why some people who have gone through emotionally intensive experiences seem to have difficulty moving forward. Therapy sometimes helps, but a session with someone trained in retrieving or healing these emotions may be just what a person needs to finally release the event and find healing.

It is not only humans who experience strong emotions!

Frantic Dog and Vengeful Father

Hubby and I once visited the home of a law enforcement officer who was experiencing a variety of unexplainable activity in the home. Upon tuning in to the energy in the home, the first thing that came to me was the presence of a large black dog. The homeowner corroborated my feeling with a story. When he had originally bought the house, it was in foreclosure. When the residents were evicted, they abandoned a large black dog inside the house, who eventually died of starvation. I was able to tune in to the spirit of the dog and escort these trapped emotions and any soul fragments left behind to the light.

Upon further investigation, I tuned in to some energy in one of his children's rooms along with some verifiable information about a person from the family's past. It turns out the homeowner's daughter had been sexually molested in that room, and the perpetrator was never prosecuted due to his mental state. The combined energy of the molestation and the anger of the father had manifested a variety of paranormal activity in his home. I suggested to the father that, in addition to a house cleansing, we do a prayer of forgiveness and release toward the perpetrator. Although the father was resistant, I explained that his anger and thoughts of helplessness and desire for revenge were hurting him and his family more than it was affecting the boy who had committed the crime. After a bit of back and forth, he was able to at least be willing to forgive and release the boy from the hatred which kept them energetically tied to one another.

Upon releasing the trapped emotions in the father's energy field, the activity stopped. All subsequent correspondence with him confirmed that the activity had never resurfaced.

There have been many books written, researched and published about how emotions become trapped in our physical bodies and create illness. I make no claims to be a doctor or therapist, nor do I ever claim that the work I do precludes a person from seeking medical or professional help. However, when I tune in to Spirit and find emotions trapped in a person's body and I am able to release those emotions, many times people report amazing results!

It is well beyond my understanding how pieces of our souls, or our life forces, become entangled in strong emotions or how those emotions become trapped in our physical bodies or physical locations, however, I do know that with the help of my Benevolent Helpers, I am able to assist many people in finding relief in their bodies and sometimes in their homes when the emotions are identified and released.

These emotions can be our own or they can be inherited from our ancestors, brought forward from a previous lifetime, acquired by accident, or even a result of an emotion that was left over from someone else! Many of us can report that we have an ancestor no one wants to acknowledge. They may have a checkered past or have done misdeeds that caused shame to the family. However, anyone in our family who is not acknowledged will at some point come back to haunt us. It may be that many generations pass and suddenly a child will begin behaving in a manner unbefitting of his upbringing. In some way, that ancestor is calling out for healing.

Just as we inherit our eye colors and our hair colors, we can inherit tendencies such as addiction problems, personality traits, mental disorders, and even depression or anger issues from those who have gone before us. Many times, I am able to detect an inherited tendency from an ancestor during a session with a client, and I assist the dead in finding resolution to the emotion or hidden event which caused a tear in the fabric of a family tapestry. Many times, the client feels a sense of release when the ancestor finds healing. In addition, the living often benefit from the healing. Those in the family who seemed to have inherited a tendency or predominant emotion for which they have no explanation seem to improve in their day to day life experience. Sometimes the improvement is not evident immediately, but over time, they notice that they are less inclined to feel sad, or angry, or a need to self-medicate.

It is a fairly foreign concept in our western thinking that those who are passed can benefit from an energy healing session, however, in my experience; I have found it to be true. At times during my meditations, I will find my family members and even the family members of friends or associates lining up, asking to be given a healing session. Often, they just want to acknowledge a trauma, or reveal a secret.

When an emotion or trauma is revealed or acknowledged, it seems to lose its power. If I do a session with a client and they do not experience an improvement in their overall life experience, then we know that we may have just scratched the surface, and there is more to heal.

Just as it is not recommended that doctors treat their own family members or law enforcement be involved in investigating family or those with whom they may have a vested interest, it is somewhat the same for the work I do. Although I desire healing for all of my clients, when the person is someone close, I sometimes find it more difficult to remain detached from the outcome. I find myself taking it personally when I do not see improvement.

Can Healing the Soul Make You Worse?

A family friend was dealing with a recurrent problem. Since she would not give me permission to attempt a healing session for her, I tuned in to her ancestors and found an ancestral pattern. I thought that if I healed the ancestors, the family line would be healed and she would have an easier time dealing with her addictions. I felt like I was successful in identifying and healing at least one ancestral pattern, however, her behavior did not improve. Each time I healed and shifted something in the spirit world, she would find herself in jail. At first, I thought that my healing work was making her worse, but, in retrospect, I surmised that perhaps each healing session on the ancestors brought her issues out in the open instead of cloaked in secrecy. In time, however, I realized that just because an ancestral pattern is healed, that does not take away free will. If a person is acting out a family pattern and the pattern is eliminated or shifted, then the person is faced with her own personal free will and her desire, or lack thereof, to seek self-improvement. Just because I heal a pattern of addiction in a family line, it does not necessarily take away the addiction in the living. The living person fighting addiction may find it easier to release the addiction, but if that person has no desire to improve, the addiction or ancestral pattern lives on, and sometimes can create anger directed at me whether or not they are aware of the healing work that has been done. It can even cause the condition of the living to get worse.

We have to realize that our lives are a combination of many factors. The initial activity, such as an addiction, can be a partial result of a family pattern, but, as we know, if two parents have multiple children, not all of them deal with the same issues. We don't necessarily inherit a family pattern just because we identify it in our ancestors. If the ancestors resolved the issue before death, it does not pass on. If I heal the pattern after they are passed, the pattern is shifted and the family line is released from the pattern. However, if a person who is living is already dealing with the pattern when the ancestors receive healing, that person is still responsible for their own choices. Those choices may not be completely the result of the family patterns. There may be more than one coal in the fire, so to speak. As a soul, they may have made an agreement with another soul involved to work on a particular issue together. They may have trapped emotions or limiting beliefs from this lifetime that contributed to the tendency to manifest the issue. They may have unresolved issues from previous lifetimes. There may be more than one family pattern at play, from more than one family line. They may have attracted the attention of non-living influences, which is a whole other problem that would fill another book!

The bottom line is that we are each responsible for our own lives and our own choices! We can do soul healings all day long, but if the recipient of those healings does not take responsibility for their own progress, and make an attempt to work on themselves, then there will most likely be limited success in any healing work that is done.

There is also the issue of taking the healing in and processing it in our hearts. We can acknowledge in our heads that we have released a burden all day long, but if we are constantly thinking about it and talking about it, then that burden is still in our hearts. Sometimes it takes years to heal our hearts even when our heads say that we have done the work.

One of the major questions I get asked is if we can do healing for our grown children without their knowledge or consent. If I cannot get the consent from the adult child from their own conscious knowledge, there is a way I can ask their soul for consent. However, sometimes the soul tells me "NO." This was the case in the aforementioned story of the girl who landed herself in jail. I tried to take a back door by doing healing with the ancestors who *did* give me consent. The ancestors were healed but the girl still maintained her own issues.

We as parents have to remember that we are responsible for raising our children the best we can and then allowing them to discover their lives on their own. They will make mistakes. They will suffer. They will end up with trapped emotions and limiting beliefs of their own, in addition to the ones they inherit. It is just a byproduct of living in the earthly realm. At some point we have to release them to make their own choices, to fall down, to choose to get up (or not). The age when we release our children to do that may be different for each child depending on the individual circumstances. But when we hold on and try to do the work for them, it may or may not yield results.

One of the best and most important things I am learning and still have to remember sometimes is that love is allowing someone to be who they are without trying to change them.

> **❝ love is allowing someone to be who they are without trying to change them. ❞**

Another largely unknown and undealt with principle is that of family loyalties. Whether we realized it or not, many of our problems can be traced back to a feeling of guilt or loyalty to a parent, a sibling, or even an unknown ancestor. We can even have unrecognized vows to religious or cultural organizations, ethnic groups, even clubs! If we have agreed to an alliance to a group, then we inherit all of the baggage of that organization. It is only through recognizing and acknowledging the loyalty, the vow, the bond, the limiting belief or trapped emotion, and then releasing it from our energy field, through intention, through ritual, through prayer, or other healing modalities, can we finally be free from the trappings of emotional, spiritual, mental and physical issues which seem to plague us.

CHAPTER FOUR

CHILDREN AND VISITS FROM THE DEAD

I have little memory of experiencing out-of-the-ordinary happenings as a child, other than my frequent nightmares, sleepwalking, and night terrors. Due to our religious beliefs, if we did experience things that were out of the ordinary, it is doubtful we would have talked about it, unless to pray.

I do know that children have more of a tendency to be open to communication with those who are not in physical form. Their hearts are open and their minds have not been contaminated by learned beliefs. Physically, their pineal glands are larger and this is commonly known as the place where psychic information is received. As we age, this gland shrinks and calcifies, making receiving psychic information more difficult. Most children cease seeing spirits about the age of six or seven, although some maintain the ability, depending on the openness of their souls and their life purposes.

The Woman Under the Ground

The most significant memory I have of sensing spirit was at about the age of five or six. My dad was an Assembly of God pastor in a tiny little town in rural Virginia. Frequently on Sundays we would go to a local park for lunch after church. I had wandered off a bit from my parents, which in the sixties was perfectly normal, I guess. Somewhere in the wooded area a woman began crying out to me from under the ground. She was crying for help to release her. This was very disconcerting to a small child, so my first instinct was to run to my parents for help. My parents obviously brushed me off, citing a child's vivid imagination. When recounting this to my mother at a later time, she confirmed that I often had vivid dreams and frequent nightmares. She maintained that this probably was one of the dreams I had, and that she had no memory of it actually happening.

Whether this memory was a dream or an actual happening, as a five-year-old, I believed it really happened. Perhaps our dreams are other rooms of reality that our souls experience while our conscious minds rest. There are reports of people who have dreams and wake with physical marks on their body representing the very experiences they had in their dreams.

Trinity and the Man At the Top of the Stairs

My granddaughter Trinity is now eight. When she was three, her other grandmother, Teresa, once called me in a panic. "I think I may need you to come and perform a cleansing on my house," she said frantically.

Teresa explained that Trinity had come running down the steps insisting that she come upstairs with her. "There is a man up there who wants to talk to you," Trinity insisted. Mistakenly thinking this was musings from the imagination of a three-year-old, Teresa followed Trinity up the stairs.

"See, there he is." Trinity pointed to the end of the upstairs hallway.

"Who is it, Trinity?" Teresa asked innocently.

"Don't you remember your own father?" Trinity asked Teresa, incredulously.

Trinity then followed up with a recounting of the place where he had died and what he had died from (heart trouble) at that very spot at the top of the stairs. Teresa was beside herself with panic. She was afraid her father was stuck in her house and that he needed assistance in crossing over.

Tuning in to her father's energy over the phone, I was able to ascertain that Teresa's father had indeed crossed over but came back periodically because he loved her and he loved the children who frequented Teresa's home. She confirmed that she and her father had been very close, and yes, he loved children.

Many times, our loved ones come back to visit, though we may rarely sense their presences or recognize the clues they may try to leave verifying their presence. When we talk about them, think about them, touch objects that belonged to them, and especially if we wear their clothes or handle belongings of theirs, their energies are drawn back into our lives. We only have to think of them to attract them back to us.

Trinity didn't stop with Teresa's father. She also claimed to have experienced Clay's brother Ray in our home and the mother of Heather, a family friend in the house where she lived with her mother for a time. She did not know that it was Heather's mother until one day Heather was going through some old pictures and showed Trinity a photo of her mother. "That is the woman who is sometimes in my room!" Trinity exclaimed.

Children, if they are nurtured and allowed to acknowledge their experiences, often have a unique ability to sense spirit. It is only the disbelief of the adults in their lives that turns off the ability. Once they reach a certain age, the ability usually goes away on its own.

Because I am my grandchildren's grandmother, they are exposed to a variety of beliefs and practices. Each of them seems to possess their own gifts in varying degrees. I attuned three of my grandchildren to the energies of Reiki and, at their request, retrieved at least one Power Animal for them. In Shamanism our Spirit Guides and Protectors often appear in the form of a familiar or perhaps not so familiar animal. It is thought that the Spirit form of animals come in order to protect us as well as provide us with guidance and assurance. Animal spirits contain "power" that is different from our own. Power animals often provide a quality or trait that we may lack in our human life experience, or reflect our personality traits or character in some way. It seems that children are very open to both Animal Spirit Guides and more human looking ones.

When Trinity reached the age of seven, the age that most children cease to see the non-living, she came to me asking me to get another Power Animal for her. I asked her why she thought she needed another one. Initially at her birth I had detected the energy of Giraffe. Giraffes have their feet on the ground and their heads in the clouds, so to speak. They teach us to live in the earthly realm but to be aware of what is happening in the upper realms as well. They teach us flexibility and adaptation to surroundings. I had told her about this one but had also gotten some other Spirit Animals for her to help her with other issues. However, I had told her that the giraffe was the one who assisted her in sensing people who were not in their bodies.

Trinity promptly reported to me, "Grandma, I need another Power Animal because Giraffe is not doing his job. I have not seen any dead people for a long time."

Obviously, when Trinity grows up, it will be her decision whether or not to reopen her ability to see dead people. Right now, she just needs to be eight and work on some other skills.

Dead Man Walking

Although we are both now in our fifties, my sister recently confessed that as a child she had seen a man and woman walking around in one of our neighboring yards. Both the man and the woman had committed suicide in that house, at different times. My sister knew that the people who she saw walking around in the yard were the souls of the deceased man and woman. She had never reported what she had seen due to our belief system. Throughout her life, she has experienced various similar experiences, but never felt free to share until I decided to come out of the "psychic closet," so to speak.

Almost anyone who has children or are around them for any significant amount of time will attest that children often report experiences that are unexplainable in our adult understanding of life. We may placate them with words like, "that is nice, sweetie." Many times, we dismiss out of hand any interactions they may have with the Spirit world, unless we are open to the idea that they may actually be able to feel, hear, see, or touch energy that we as adults are not privy to.

As we adults become more aware of the subtle shifts in energy that occur when the presence of Spirit is near, maybe we will realize that the skill has been dormant in us since we were children and that those tiny humans in our lives have innate skills we have forgotten or stuffed down due to the need to conform to society and function in a world that marginalizes the out of the ordinary.

CHAPTER FIVE

WHAT HAPPENS WHEN WE DIE? THE UNQUIET GRAVE

B rought up a born-again Christian, I was taught that when you died, you either went to Heaven or Hell. It didn't totally matter how good of a person you were. The real ticket to Heaven was whether or not you had accepted Jesus as your savior. If you were a mass murderer or a serial rapist and in your last breath you asked for forgiveness from Jesus, then when you died, the Angels would come and carry you home the same way they would if you had spent your life doing good.

This belief has obvious flaws. What about people who had never heard of Jesus? This was the motivation for centuries of Christians going about the world and dragging people away from their belief systems and converting them to Christianity. So they say. As I have previously discussed, when I tune in to the world of Spirit and specifically to the dead, I have not found that the souls are in one of two places, Heaven or Hell. I have never once tuned in to a soul in Hell. On what I call the "other side," it seems there are many different layers of reality and I tend to find souls in many different places, but what was described to me in church was almost never there.

This belief in being "saved" also abdicates personal responsibility, of which I am an advocate. But I am not here to argue the validity of that belief. I am here to tell the story of my Higher Guidance and what they told me when I asked them. I should preface this chapter with a little explanation of what I currently believe about my Higher Guidance System.

In no way do I think for a minute that the information I receive when I am in meditation or deeper states of awareness comes from me in my normal waking consciousness. However, I do believe that on some deep level we are all connected to one another and that we are all connected to Higher Wisdom that we do not normally access on a day to day, moment to moment basis. We can call this wisdom Jesus, God, Goddess, the Holy Spirit, Allah, Shakti, Angels, or any number of other names.

When I connect to Higher Wisdom, I can feel the energy of various beings coming in to my awareness while in an altered state of consciousness. Whether this is my own Higher Wisdom that is connecting to the Divine Wisdom while presenting itself to me as a frog or a goddess or a shaman, I am not here to argue. I will address that point in a moment with the information they shared with me as I connected to the Higher Wisdom that talks to me.

Four Spirits Talk About Death

Believe it or not, it wasn't until recently that I asked my Guides what really happens when we die. I wanted to address the belief in crossing over souls, which I will cover later, but I soon realized that the information they presented to me filled a chapter entirely on its own.

That morning I had drawn my daily tarot card and I had drawn the four of Cups. The picture on the card is of a man sitting under a tree with his arms crossed. There is a hand coming out of the clouds holding a cup and there are three cups sitting in front of him. Since my interpretation of the cards change depending on the information Spirit provides, I had an idea that I was going to be receiving guidance from four Guides. I knew I had to connect that day and the information was important.

I am also not here to argue the concept of Guides. This is the information that came to me, in the order it was received, as I sat in meditation. In simple terms, when I say "Guides," I am talking about the Higher Wisdom that speaks to me when I am quiet and listening.

The first Guide that presented himself was my Shaman Guide. He is Native American, an older man, who sometimes wears that headdress with all the feathers. Sometimes I don't really see him, but I feel him and the color red is normally present. I always feel I am going to receive some profound wisdom or sometimes he comes when I am seeing clients to bring information or healing.

...the three worlds

He reminded me that in shamanism there is the belief in the three worlds. There is the upper world, the middle world, and the lower world. Each of these worlds represents a different realm of consciousness and an alternate dimension where we go to find wisdom or retrieve lost pieces of people's essences or souls.

He told me that one of the reasons the Native Americans would place their dead high up in structures they built specifically for the dead was in hopes they would have an easier transition to the upper world. One of my previous-life memories that I accidently accessed during a guided meditation was of being on that structure looking down on my loved ones from that life time and feeling very emotional. In that memory I turned into a white bird and flew away. But that is another story.

My Guide told me that when a soul leaves its body, it goes to one of the three worlds. It is mostly a choice based on that soul's state of consciousness at the time. Knowing that when I am in altered states of consciousness and going to the place where I travel into the three worlds, normally I am led into one of the three as though I am being sucked in there by a vacuum cleaner. I wouldn't have thought of the experience as a choice I was making myself. However, my guide said that our state of consciousness is a choice. Therefore, we also have the choice to experience the world we want to enter, although it may not really be a conscious decision.

For example, it has been said that here in the West some of our beliefs would not hold water in third world countries. Would you attempt to talk about the Law of Attraction to a community where there was no running water or the main goal was obtaining the next meal? This is a more complicated scenario! How could someone actually chose to live in those conditions? We will not spend a lot of time contemplating the choices that a starving person made or whether or not it was a choice in the first place. However, I think we can agree that a person in those circumstances would not consciously choose to live in those circumstances over living in an abundant community. If we use that example to show that the state of mind and the individual experiences of a soul while in their bodies would determine their "choice" of what happens after they die, we can see that even though we think that when we die we will choose to go to what the shamans call the "upper world" and Christians call "Heaven," we can't say for certain that we will be in a place emotionally and mentally to make that sort of choice.

It stands to reason that souls that "choose" not to cross into the upper world but choose the middle world are the ones that are still here or are in some proximity to Earth but in a different experience of the earthly realm than we who still reside in physical bodies are experiencing. Just as if we embark upon a journey that is supposed to take us from New York City to San Francisco, at any point on that journey we will find ourselves somewhere in between. So, at the point of death, our souls may very well be experiencing what we can only say is a journey from living in a physical body to whatever is next.

My Shaman Guide also talked about praying for the deceased. This is a practice in Catholicism as well, where they light candles for the dead. He told me that honoring the ancestors and seeking their wisdom was preferred, rather than seeking the guidance of deities. Our ancestors are connected to us through blood and love us personally. As I previously discussed, if we have ancestors with less than savory pasts, praying for them assists them in going into higher levels of the upper world. However, this practice also blesses us because when our ancestors ascend, we ascend with them. No matter how unsavory our ancestors may have been, we should bless them and honor them. If we find ourselves unable to do that, then we should not dishonor them by talking negatively about them or attempting to remove their life from the family tree. Instead, we should remove the thoughts of them from our minds and exist completely without any emotional ties to them whatsoever.

This can also be applied to the larger picture of world history. It seems that when we become more aware of misconduct by our ancestors, we attempt to remove any mention of them from history books or even tear down or disfigure statues erected at a different time in history to honor them. We have to remember that removing a statue does not erase the history. When we dishonor those who are an important part of our history, we dishonor the part they played in the life we now live. Yes, let us learn from history. Yes, let us attempt to be better humans and to be kind and accepting of one another. But let us not think that when we remove a person from our family or national or even world history that we remove the effects that took place as a result of that history.

Years ago, Spirit told me that we cannot heal a wound without attempting to heal both the victim and the perpetrator. There are more than two sides to every story. Each of us is doing the best we can given the knowledge and understanding we have at any moment in our lives. I am not saying we should not call those who have behaved shamefully into acknowledging or paying for their crimes. But we do not have to follow them down the same path by our emotional connection to them. If we do not acknowledge those in our family history or in our world history as being a piece of the puzzle of our lives, in some way that behavior is guaranteed to come back at some point to be included. We cannot exclude members of our family or world tree without expecting that at some point in the future that void will be filled.

In this session with my Shaman Guide, he did not specify how long a soul may be in any one of the three worlds, or give me any details as to what the living can do to assist the dead in reconciling their life experiences and their connections to the living and moving on. However, I have been privileged to have assisted the dead on this journey and, in the process, have gained some perspective.

...consciousness is like an ocean

The next Guide who stepped forward was my Buddhist Guide. The color red is also present with him but there is a different feel to his energy. He told me to think of consciousness as the ocean. The ocean is filled with individual drops of water that together make the whole. When we come into our bodies, we focus our awareness on being an individual drop of water. Sometimes we forget that we are a single drop in an ocean of awareness, and that we are connected to all the other drops of water that collectively make up the ocean. By tuning in to the awareness of another drop of water, we can receive information and transmit thoughts and words from the individualization of that other drop of water. That is why Spirit communication is possible. Together we create the ocean of awareness. Individually we experience life, death, and myriad other events. When we die, we go back to the ocean of consciousness from which we came. Depending on our experiences while focusing our attention on being a drop of water, we may not immediately go back to the ocean of awareness but may still maintain some of our individualization. Just as some of the drops of water in the ocean are floating at the top feeling the sunshine and the rain, perhaps bouncing around up in the air at times or splashing around with other drops of water, some are sitting near the ocean floor in total darkness, surrounded by sand, and mixing with all the other energy forms that settle near the bottom. Our experiences of being a drop of water in an ocean of awareness may be different but we are all part of the ocean and without us there would be no ocean.

...our thoughts and beliefs create our experience of the afterlife

The third Guide who presented herself was a relatively new Guide to me. I had actually researched her and called her when I found a kitten on the side of the road one day while I was running. With the help of my husband, we rescued this tiny little ball of fluff, complete with sharp claws and teeth, and brought her home. At first, having her was like having a fur ball with needles and pins sticking out of her feet. She would not allow us to touch her and she would not eat. She kept disappearing and we were not even anticipating accepting her as a full-time resident in our home. Then I remembered that there was an Egyptian goddess named Bast who was the goddess of cats. I called upon her to assist us in calming this scared little ball of fur and filling her with the assurance that we meant her no harm. Bast appears to me as a dark figure, tall and beautiful. Sometimes the only thing I can see are her eyes, much like our little black kitty.

The morning I called Bast, I asked her to assist us in taming her and getting the kitten to eat. I headed out to work and went about my business. My husband called around noon and told me that he had found the kitten and she had come to him calmly and allowed him to feed her. She is now a beloved member of our family.

Bast told me that our thoughts, beliefs, and words create what we experience. Just as she had come to me after I had called out to her for assistance, she told me that centuries ago when many more people believed in her, she enjoyed a more powerful presence than she now exhibits. The qualities that people attributed to her would be the qualities those people would experience. The more people who believed in her, talked to her, talked about her, and felt her presence, the more powerful she became.

She told me that when we die, it is the same. The thoughts and beliefs we have about death and dying become what we experience after death, at least for a time. If someone believes that they have been bad and deserve to go to Hell, then they may experience, at least for a time until that belief changes, a place resembling Hell. If they believe in the Golden Gates and the Angels welcoming them home, then they will have an experience resembling that.

If someone passes with no particular belief about life or death, then there are many different possibilities of what they may experience. If they are worried about their loved ones, or die under traumatic circumstances, their consciousness could possibly remain in the earth realm.

Bast also reminded me of a concept I had become aware of since my experiences with talking to the dead. She wanted me to remember that the thoughts and emotions of the people who knew the deceased also affect their ability to go on to the next adventure of their soul. Many souls are stuck in the in-between world due to the grief of those who love them. There is a little-known concept that seems to hold true: A person does not truly die until no one remembers them. I don't think that means that famous people never truly move on if we remember them forever. I think it means the people who knew them and either loved or hated the person that they were.

I happened upon a poem, written anonymously a couple of hundred years ago, that describes a possible conversation that a man and his deceased lover had after her death.

The Unquiet Grave
BY ANONYMOUS

"The wind doth blow today, my love,
And a few small drops of rain;
I never had but one true-love,
In cold grave she was lain.

"I'll do as much for my true-love
As any young man may;
I'll sit and mourn all at her grave
For a twelvemonth and a day."

The twelvemonth and a day being up,
The dead began to speak:
"Oh who sits weeping on my grave,
And will not let me sleep?"

"'T is I, my love, sits on your grave,
And will not let you sleep;
For I crave one kiss of your clay-cold lips,
And that is all I seek."

"You crave one kiss of my clay-cold lips,
But my breath smells earthy strong;
If you have one kiss of my clay-cold lips,
Your time will not be long.

"'T is down in yonder garden green,
Love, where we used to walk,
The finest flower that e're was seen
Is withered to a stalk.

"The stalk is withered dry, my love,
So will our hearts decay;
So make yourself content, my love,
Till God calls you away."

When we spend a long time grieving over a loved one, we are not doing them any favors. They remain tied to us through an invisible cord of energy that brings them back into our experience. This is what many people experience as hauntings in the paranormal realm. Someone they love has passed and they experience various forms of connection. Sometimes this can be the deceased simply assuring their loved ones that they are okay on the other side. But if the emotions are deep and felt on a regular basis, then, at some point, the living need to release the deceased to go on to the next experience of their soul.

Holding on to them due to grief is okay in the beginning, but when it lasts for years it becomes selfish. We are contributing to the soul remaining in the in-between place, or in shamanism, the middle world. I have received this message from deceased loved ones and pets on more than one occasion. I was surprised when they told me that they were stuck between worlds because the living would not let them go.

In shamanism it is believed that when a soul who was formerly not at rest, or "stuck" is assisted to the other side, whether through the process of crossing over or through other means, the story of the crossing should not be talked about or thought about after that, so as to prevent the soul from being brought back. In my connection to my Guides, they told me to wait at least a year in Earth time before speaking or thinking of that crossing. Although time does not exist on the other side, after a year in Earth time there is less of a cord of energy tying the deceased to the event of the crossing. They have had time to acclimate on the other side and there is less chance that they will be brought back. This ties back to Bast telling me that our thoughts, beliefs, and words have power and create what we experience. On an energetic level, we have more power than we realize.

This is one of the reasons why in this day and age of ghost tours and our focus on hauntings and paranormal experiences, we have to be careful what we think, say, and believe. We may be creating the very experiences of which we are being told. There may not have been the ghost of the evil caretaker of the orphanage before the ghost tours started, but taking groups of people through the building five times a day and telling the story may have caused the energy of the evil woman to be brought back, if not her specifically.

In recent months our collective experience as humanity has been ravaged by a killer virus. Souls are leaving the earth realm in record numbers. Funerals have become taboo or even prohibited. Those who are left grieving and those who are leaving their bodies are left without closure.

I had become aware of the unrest in the astral planes early on in the experience of the virus. Spirit gave me a blessing to say to those who were gathered collectively in the land of the dead so that they could move on. I share this blessing with you. Feel free to use this blessing as you see fit as you bless the ones you love and the ones you come across who need closure. This blessing frees the living and the dead from their unfinished business and gives them permission to move on to the next expression of their souls.

9 Blessings

1. We bless you for your life. We bless your contribution to our lives, through your love, your choices, your words, thoughts and actions. Even the ones that you or I may view as less than helpful, we bless those too. We bless the way you chose to experience life in this particular incarnation of your soul.

2. We release you from any emotions that would hold you through obligation to the living. We bless you as you leave your physical body to the next expression of your soul. Although we feel sadness and loss and grief as you pass on to the next adventure, we bless you as you move on to the next thing, whatever that may be.

3. We bless you as you greet those who have gone before you. We welcome in to your transition those who love you who have come to greet you and lead you into the next realm of awareness. We ask that the highest available Beings of Love and Light, be they Angels, Guides, loving Ancestors, or Deities who you have aligned yourself with during life, greet you and lead you on to the next plane of existence.

4. We bless you by releasing your body back to nature in the way that you have chosen or in the way that best represents the return of your physical existence back to the earth who supported you in life and provided you with food, water, air, and breath. We release your physical body existence and we release your soul from any cord that would try to stay connected to physical body existence.

5. We bless you as you navigate this huge change and transition in your awareness. We understand that it may take a little time to settle in to this new expression of your soul and we embrace the changes with you as we also change the way we experience your soul and your contribution to our lives. We will need some time as we process the grief and loss at your passing and understand that you may need a little time as well.

6. We bless the way you experienced your physical body awareness and expression of life in the way you connected to us individually and collectively. We bless the relationship we shared with you and the new relationship to your energy and the memory of our lives together. We remember the love, the joy, the tears, the sadness, the conversations, the times of silence or difficulty or separation. We bless the good times we shared and the challenges we faced either together or individually. We understand and acknowledge that none of us ever lives our lives free from regret or bad choices. We bless all the interactions we had, both the happy ones and the challenging ones, for they created opportunities for greater awareness and understanding.

7. We bless you for the path you chose in life. We bless all the bumps on the road, all the delays or detours that may have carried you in directions we loved and directions we objected to or did not understand. We acknowledge that your life was your own, and you navigated it in the best way that you could given the way that your path unfolded for you.

8. We bless and acknowledge the gifts you gave to us in life. Every action that resulted in a change in our relationship to you, whether it turned out to be beneficial or challenging, we acknowledge that every word you spoke, every action you took that affected us in one way or another, every expression of love or less than love, each breath you took was a gift to us in some way. Your life changed the way we experienced life. We thank you for your presence in our life.

9. We bless this ending of our physical relationship to one another. We acknowledge that every ending precedes a new beginning. Although the way we experience one another is changing, our relationship to one another will always be an aspect of the growth of our soul. We will always be in some way tied to one another through our memories, our awareness, and our connection. Whether we experience life together or apart, we will always be in some way a part of one another's journey of awareness and

experience. We bless you and release you to the Light of Divine Love and Light.

In my interactions with my Guides who explained to me what happens when we die, I mentioned that according to the tarot card that indicated to me that a transmission was coming, there should have been four Guides. I connected with three and related the wisdom they shared, but what about the fourth?

...distractions!

I asked about that and I heard the voice of a British woman who did not identify herself. At the time I was busy straightening up the house for some expected visitors and we chatted a bit about the information the other three Guides had shared with me. She made the observation that none of the information that came through contradicted any of the other information I had acquired. Each transmission was a different way of looking at the same subject; each Guide had presented a different aspect of the answer to the question I had posed. The Shaman Guide had shared with me the concept of the three worlds and how souls when they passed crossed into one of these three worlds. The Buddhist Guide had shared the concept of the ocean and how our soul could be compared to one drop of water in an ocean of consciousness. Bast, the Egyptian Goddess of cats shared with me how our perceptions and beliefs formulate our experiences, both during our time in our physical bodies and after our consciousness leaves our body.

As I was busy cleaning while chatting with this British woman, I did not stop to write down our conversation. Later when I tried to bring it back or recall what was said, I drew a blank. The lesson in my interaction with her was perhaps the importance of recording or writing down conversations with the non-living. When their presence is gone, the information they shared can also be gone with them.

In thinking back to the tarot card image that told me there were to be four messages, three interactions were concrete and real, and one was a bit vague. In the picture on the card, three cups are sitting in front of the man on the ground and one is up in the air held by a hand coming out of the clouds. Spirit specifically told me ahead of time that three interactions would be direct and one would be a bit less concrete.

CHAPTER SIX

TRUSTING THE INFORMATION

S ince I started listening to Spirit and teaching others to tune in to their own intuitive abilities, I have learned that the main hurdle to overcome is trust. When we first start being open to receiving information, it is easy to wonder whether we are just imagining things or if the information is accurate. I would guess that many, if not most of us, have received important guidance or communication from Spirit that we have dismissed or not recognized as interaction from Spirit. Many times, the information seems to contradict what we may think or believe. I am sure that in the early days, there were countless times I received information but discounted it as my own thoughts or imagination. However, the more I opened up to Spirit and conveyed the messages that I received, the more I began to trust the information I was receiving.

I guess in a way I was a rebel in my former belief system. Many times, I questioned the things that were being taught as 'gospel' truth. This undoubtedly affected my relationship with those in power and resulted in the pastor forbidding me from giving messages in the church. I think I got this from my mother, who was a very devoted Christian but also had a reputation for questioning authority. This gave me a bit of an advantage when Spirit began telling me things that did not fit into my belief system.

Sometimes the messages we receive are fairly insignificant, but Spirit often tests us to see if we will listen.

When Spirit Whispers

Before I retired, I had a habit of sitting in my car and meditating for a bit before going in to work. One morning, after my morning meditation, I began gathering my thoughts and preparing to go inside and get ready to go to work. I was contemplating leaving my bag in the car and only taking inside a few choice necessities. I looked into my bag to decide what I wanted, and a small bottle of pain reliever seemed to attract my attention. I contemplated taking it inside, but decided against it, since I was feeling fine and my hands were already full.

Within minutes of arriving, my boss asked me if I had any pain reliever. Aha! Okay, so I had to go back out to my car and retrieve the bottle of pills. *Okay, Spirit. Next time I will listen.*

Is the Light Hot???

I really don't relish going into locations which used to house the insane or hardened criminals. I am not sure what the attraction is, but this seems to be a popular scenario for those who enjoy investigating the paranormal. On one occasion Clay was successful in enticing me to join him on a visit to a location which at one time in its history was a hospital, where the patients were apparently mistreated. This happened to be one of those events where the paranormal investigators would gather and set up tables, sell their books, offer their services, and then later do an investigation of the location.

Clay and I have a habit of arriving early to every event we attend and this day was no exception. The coordinator of the event was there and we were there, but none of the other vendors had yet arrived. The person coordinating the event asked if we would like a one-on-one tour of the property and we agreed. I often find that locations are contaminated with the energy of the living who are nearby, which makes picking up information difficult, so I found this tour preferable to one where there were a lot of living people.

Room by room, the event facilitator led us around this enormous building. In one of the rooms, I encountered the energy of an older woman in a hospital bed. I perceived that her soul needed to cross over, and that her emotions of despair and anger hung heavily in the room. She was extremely angry at her doctor, who had apparently shackled her in her bed and given her painful injections of some kind. The anger was the emotion that was keeping her stuck. She related to me that she hoped her doctor burned in hell for the torture he had put her through. Nevertheless, I knew she could find peace in the light. I tried to encourage her to go to the light but she shrieked, "NO! The light is hot and I am afraid!"

I had never heard any spirits convey to me a fear that the light was hot, so I was a bit confused. How can a soul be afraid that the light is hot? I am not sure if she went to the light or not. We cannot cross free will and if a soul does not want to go, we cannot force them.

When other mediums began to arrive, I asked a couple of them if they had ever heard that from a soul before. They all said they had not. Trusting the communication, I asked Spirit to give me some confirmation that the information was accurate.

Upon returning home, I picked up one of my many books and opened to a random page. This is often how I receive information from Spirit. In that particular book, on the page to which I had turned, I read that when a soul is connected to dark energy which some call demons, that energy will convince them that the light is hot. This is what keeps them stuck in the darkness.

Many years before, when I left the church, the idea of demons and the devil were placed on the shelf with many of my other beliefs. I did not have the experience of running in to them often since I had left the church, although within the church we often blamed the devil for a lot of the bad things that happened. I had since decided that I really didn't know if the devil or demons existed, but this was not an area in which I wanted to focus. Maybe they are real, maybe they aren't, but they aren't affecting me, so I will leave that to someone else to explore. However, in this instance, I had come into contact with a message from Spirit that seemed to confirm their existence through the passage in that particular book. That information has since aided me in assisting energy to go to the light, and, on occasion, I have been able to assist even the dark energy in going to the light.

The point is I trusted the information, even though I did ask for additional information from my Guides to verify the communication. Asking for additional information is always honored by Spirit.

Is Mom Ok?

On another occasion, a woman came to me who was sensitive and who was able to physically see and communicate with Spirit, but she was upset because a month previously her mother had passed and she had been unable to connect with her. She was worried about her mother and wanted to see if I could connect with her. At the time I happened to be working my day job. I worked at the front counter waiting on customers, and the woman knew what I did "on the side." The woman's mother immediately presented herself. I felt the normal rush of energy when Spirit shows up and my heart began to race. After looking around to make sure no one was watching, I connected with her mother. She told me that she did not realize it had been a month since her passing. She said she had been asleep in the hospital since her passing, which seemed odd to me. I was not aware at that time that there is a hospital on the other side or that souls needed to sleep, but I conveyed the information. I also sensed that she had not been herself for a while and may have been in and out of awareness while in her body. The daughter agreed with my assessment. She told me that her mother had dementia in her last years and that she had experienced difficulty sleeping toward the end. It made perfect sense to her that her mother may not have had a sense of time and that she may have been sleeping or recovering on the other side from the difficulty of her last years on earth.

If I had not trusted the information that I received, the woman's daughter would not have received the information she needed from her mother, or the assurance that her mother was okay on the other side.

Sometimes I think we have the idea that once someone passes, they are a wealth of information and that they will know things they did not know while in their bodies. This is not normally the case. If they were a cad in this life, they are probably still a cad, although I do hope they are working on that in some way.

We also have the idea that when a person passes, they are off floating on a cloud or that everything is wonderful and they are immediately healed of all their ills. It has been my revelation after connecting with many souls that there is a period of recovery and evaluation of their life. Those whose lives ended abruptly or in a difficult manner may have been so shocked at the experience that a number of things may have occurred. They may not realize they are dead. They may have not yet crossed over. They may still be in a fog (this often happens when people die of drug overdoses). They may not want to tell their living loved ones the truth of what happened.

When allowing the Higher Beings to speak through my voice, I am still mostly aware of what they are saying, and I still maintain control, where I can say, "Okay this is enough, I am done." I will say that sometimes I wish someone would write down what they say, because it is difficult to recall it later. It is kind of like listening to someone talk on television. I am not the one coming up with the information, so I tend to forget if it is not recorded or written down.

The Disappearing Angel

In the early days I had asked some friends to allow me to channel for them as a way of practicing my skills. A friend had come over and I was channeling an Angel. The friend could ask questions of the Angel and the Angel would answer.

My friend asked the Angel where something was in the house, and I heard the Angel say, "Wait a minute while I go look and I will be right back." I heard the Angel say this, and immediately thought, *wait a minute, don't Angels know everything? Why does she have to go look?* (I say *she* but Angels aren't really male or female; they just present themselves that way.)

Anyway, the Angel was gone. I felt her leave and she did not come back. My friend, who also happens to be sensitive, felt her leave. I thought that the reason she left was that she sensed my questioning the communication and it cut off the connection. It was almost like doubt during communication resembled a kink in a water hose. Immediately, there is no more water. I have subsequently found that on other occasions when I doubt the communication, the link is lost.

Trusting the communication is vital to the continuation of the session. I am not saying that you cannot question the communication. It is okay to ask questions, to ask for clarification or even confirmation. It is okay to ask that the information or instruction be verified or to ask for additional signs or for validating information to come forth as evidence. This is different than doubting. I don't believe Spirit wants us to just believe everything they say. However, when we doubt what we are receiving is coming from Spirit, or we are afraid that the information is coming from our own imaginations, that is like turning off the signal.

Over time, we will learn the voice of Spirit. We recognize the energy. It is like talking to an old friend. Even when we are communicating something and the person to whom we are communicating does not understand or validate the information, we have to trust that we are hearing correctly. If the communication does not resonate with the person, I normally just tell them to stick it in the freezer and take it out later.

Mom and Her Candles

A recent seeker came to me and I was able to connect with her mother. At some point in the session I saw candles. Normally when I see candles in a reading it means it is someone's birthday or a significant event. The seeker could not think of an upcoming birthday or anniversary but remarked that her mother used to paint and one of the things she liked to paint was candles. This is one of many instances when the deceased show me a picture of something but it is up to us to figure out what it means.

Spirit will only tell us what we can handle. I am sure there are universes of information in the Spirit world that our Guides have not yet shared with us. In time, we will understand everything.

I am one of those spirit communicators who likes to go to other spirit communicators for messages. Yes, I can hear for myself, but it is harder when the information I am looking for is something that I have an emotional attachment to. In order to be an effective spirit communicator, I need to be objective. I need to be open to whatever the communication might be. I have to not be resistant to the messages I may receive.

Making Mistakes

I had gotten close to a girlfriend of one of the members of my immediate family. I really wanted her to be *the one*. She was open to my gift and would often ask me to give her messages from Spirit. I should have known better. I did tell her that I did not make a habit of reading friends and family members if the information is something that I wanted to be a certain way. I really liked her.

You guessed it. There was a bad breakup and the messages turned out to be inaccurate. I hear you. If I am a spirit communicator, why did I not know the relationship would end badly? I really don't know. Perhaps I did know on some level but I was hoping the outcome would be different. Spirit does not tell me everything. Perhaps I was resistant to the information because of my emotional attachment to her.

If you want to make friends with a medium so you can have all-day, every-day access to Spirit messages, I am sorry to break this to you, but it doesn't work that way. Once you become my friend, I will most likely not give you messages unless the spirit world is really insistent. I have one story where Spirit would not leave me alone until I delivered a message to an ex-family member.

My Ex-Mother-In-Law and the Dying Plant

I was remarried, and the divorce from my first husband had not been a friendly one. My current husband owned a health food store at the time of this story. I had placed a few choice objects in the store. One of them was a beautiful wooden table that my ex-father-in-law had made. On top of it sat a plant. Hubby Clay had many plants in the store, and most of them predated my presence in his life. This plant was no exception. It had always been a healthy, happy plant.

One evening hubby and I had gone to the movies. After the movies we had stopped by the store and it was dark and empty. We walked in and the first thing I noticed was the plant sitting on the table built by my ex-father-in-law. The plant was near death. It had really started failing since my last visit to the store. Immediately I received the message that my ex-father-in-law was about to pass. I had not had any contact with the family and would have no reason to know any information about them. A few years back my ex's mother and aunt had passed and they were the ones whose presence I felt giving me the message. I felt sad about my ex's dad and his mother and aunt were insistent that I communicate to my ex that he needed to go visit his father. I argued with them.

They knew how strained our relationship was. They knew he did not believe in what I do now, but they did not care. Hmm. Conundrum.

So, I hatched a plan. I called my daughter and told her she needed to, first of all, check on her grandfather. Then she needed to call her father and somehow get him to go visit his father. What I found out was that my daughter's grandfather was indeed in the hospital and all attempts to get certain family members to visit him had been met with failure. Apparently, she had been left out of the loop and didn't even know her grandfather was sick.

Because of the dynamics of that family, I decided to go visit him myself. We had enjoyed a good relationship when his son and I were together. I expected it to go well, and it did. I showed him pictures of his grandchild and great-grandchildren, we made small talk, and I said goodbye.

My daughter was finally successful in getting her dad to his father's bedside. The morning he left to go back home; his father passed.

Some souls are waiting to resolve unfinished business before they feel ready to move on. Apparently, this was the case for my ex-father-in-law.

Sometimes the information that comes through is a bit out of the ordinary. I received the information of my ex-father-in-law's impending passing based on an observation of a plant sitting on a table he had made. I trusted the information and it turned out to be accurate. He was able to pass without leaving any unfinished business. And no one was the wiser (unless this certain someone reads this book, which is unlikely).

Recently my ex-mother-in-law appeared to me again, this time asking me to attempt to heal the broken relationship my daughter had with her father. I contacted my daughter, and she reluctantly got in touch with her father. It turns out that he had recently suffered a health scare, and was facing his own mortality.

Relationships are complicated. Sometimes my gift as a medium stirs up some unresolved and perhaps unhealed wounds in my own life or in the lives of my closest family and friends. I never assume a loved one appearing to me from the other side is there to predict the impending death of a close friend or relative, despite that being the case on occasion. I will never tell someone that a loved one (or not so loved one) is about to die. That is up to the souls themselves.

I did tell my daughter to find some closure and make amends with her dad, if that was possible, but to have boundaries and maintain her ground on unresolved issues. I advised her to listen to her gut. If the relationship was complicated and there were issues which couldn't be worked out, let them go. I wanted her to do the best she could.

Messages from the Living

Occasionally when I am giving a reading, a soul who is not on the other side will come to give a message to a client. At first, I did not know this was possible. When the souls come to me, I do not always know whether they are in their physical body or not, but I sense the energy. In the beginning when a soul came to me, I assumed they were on the other side, but I soon found this was not always the case.

Recently I was reading a client and I heard the word "father." In this reading we were not specifically talking to the dead, but were resolving issues with past relationships, so I had no reason to question the information. However, the client remarked that she really didn't have any issues with her father, that they had a good relationship.

Nevertheless, I confirmed that the soul coming through to me was her father through some information that he provided. I asked the client if her father had ever given her a hard time about some of her choices. She confirmed that he had. I also sensed that her father was too proud to apologize in real life and instead, showed his love for his daughter through actions, not words. She confirmed this also. Her father came through to tell her that he did want to apologize for giving her a hard time in the past. He wanted her to know he loved her and would always support her choices, although he may never express that to her face to face.

The client then asked if her mother had any messages for her. Her mother also was alive and she had just spoken to her before our session. I told her that her mother was smiling and saying, "Hang in there. Things will get better." The client exclaimed that those were the very words her mother had said to her before she came to see me.

Over time, a relationship is developed with the Spirit world. I am given images, words, phrases, lyrics to a song, scenes from a movie. It is almost like a cat chasing a string. I am given a string and I have to follow it to get the whole story.

Oil of Oregano

Sometime before I retired from the Post Office, I woke up to a bit of a scratchy throat and stuffy nose. "I don't have time for this!" I exclaimed to Spirit. Being a spirit communicator and a wedding Officiant, not to mention my 8 to 5 job at the Post Office, I would often find I had little time to be sick or to just sit and *be*. I frequently arrived at work twenty minutes early to have my meditation time in the car and I would try to schedule clients around my trips to the gym and my family time, but sometimes I would find I was booked pretty solid.

This particular week I had my regular job, a wedding rehearsal and wedding, and three clients scheduled. I couldn't just call a bride and say, "Sorry I can't make it; I have a cold."

The morning of the rehearsal I had taken the day off work at the Post Office and decided to sleep in. In that early morning in-between state when you are not sure if you are awake or asleep, I heard *oil of oregano*. Despite the fact that I am married to a man who owned a health food store for over twenty years, I am not really an expert on natural remedies. Whenever I would present with symptoms, hubby would just hand me a pill or a drink and say, "Here, take this."

I had no prior knowledge of what oil of oregano was used for or if you could take it internally. This was my string. So, I got up, went to Google on my computer, and typed the question: "what is oil of oregano used for." I found that some people claim it can be used as a natural antibiotic and it is known for helping with respiratory issues. There were also instructions for how much to take and how often. I opened up our cabinet and found, lo and behold, a bottle of oil of oregano.

Hearing the words *oil of oregano* was the string. I had to follow it and do a little leg work on my own. Spirit didn't tell me to place a drop of the oil under my tongue or that it was good for respiratory issues.

Color Blind Kitty

Another time I was tuning in to my kitty, trying to see if there was anything she wanted to tell me. I do not exclusively do pet communication but I have had some success in this area so she seemed like a good guinea pig. When I tuned in to her, I could see things through her eyes. Everything was different shades of blue. *My kitty is colorblind!* Upon coming back into present time, I once again visited Google and asked if cats are colorblind. The answer was that cats do not see reds and yellows, only shades of blue and green.

Tea Leaves or Cinnamon?

I am always trying to learn new and fun methods of divination, just to add some variety to my little basket of tricks. Recently I decided to give a go at tea leaf reading.

I drink my tea with the tea inside the bags, which won't work with traditional tea leaf reading, but on many occasions, I like to sprinkle some cinnamon in my tea. One morning I was sitting out on my patio and was just about done with my tea. I had a thought: *I wonder if I can read the cinnamon in the bottom of my teacup.*

There was just a little bit of liquid in the bottom of the cup, and I swished it around the cup nine times like the book said, so that the cinnamon could create a pattern on the inside of the teacup.

When I looked inside the cup, I saw two mountains, what appeared to be a bunch of faces above the mountains, some people below, and a road that went through the mountains.

"Oh well," I thought to myself, "it is my first try. Maybe I will try again later sometime."

The next day I was reading for a new client. Near the end of the session, she asked if she could tell me what she saw one day when she was in a car accident and had an out of body experience.

You guessed it. She rose above the road where the accident happened. She saw two mountains. She saw a bunch of faces up in the clouds and people below. She saw a road going through the mountains that she knew led to her grandmother's house.

Next time I read the cinnamon in my cup; I am taking a picture of it.

Perhaps the biggest key to effective and accurate communication with Spirit is believing the messages I receive. Sometimes the information may seem a little off, and sometimes clients can claim they don't know what I am talking about. And yes, sometimes I am wrong. But I always trust what I receive. I may interpret the message incorrectly and, depending on which spirit I am talking to, sometimes the spirits themselves may lie, but I always trust what I hear.

CHAPTER SEVEN

TALKING TO THE DEAD

Talking to the dead was not my original specialty. In my former belief system, I was taught that a soul when he or she died went to one of two places: heaven or hell. It was forbidden in the Old Testament to attempt to contact the dead, although there is that story of one of the kings of Israel contacting a medium to talk to a dead prophet, who actually showed up and talked to him! And then there was the story of Jesus and how he connected to Moses and one of the prophets who actually showed up in physical form for Jesus' disciples to see and recognize.

In my upbringing, talking to the dead was forbidden, and anyone who did was thought to be talking to the devil pretending to be a dead person. It was thought that once you died, there was a great divide that separates the living and the dead and it could not be crossed until you died.

Despite the fact that my belief system had denied the possibility of ghosts or connecting with the dead, I had unexplained events in every house I lived in. Most of the time I would discount the events or try to explain them away. My daughter, however, was a believer and had many experiences which she never shared with me until many years later when I began to open up to the possibility of paranormal activity. My sister would frequently see spirits and, as I mentioned before, even saw the spirit of a woman and a man walking around in the yard who had committed suicide in the house across the street. She never shared her experiences due to our belief system and was relieved when I re-acquainted myself with the ability to sense spirits.

Initially, I was open to the possibility of ghosts and talking to the dead. Clay's brother Ray had indeed showed up at our home. I was aware of his presence but never really tried to talk to him at first. I did find, on occasion, that I would connect with those who had passed. It was not a service I offered to the public but when it was asked for, I was happy to communicate.

Joe

Early on, before I admitted to myself that I could talk to the dead, I believed the communication was just my imagination. A good friend and colleague passed away at a time when I was just beginning to suspect I *could* talk to the dead. I went to his funeral. He was Catholic and a good bit of our time together was spent talking about the differences in our belief systems. At the time of our friendship, I was still deep into my Christian beliefs. He liked to talk to St. Francis about his animals and I was incredulous that people actually prayed to someone other than Jesus. I remember saying to him, "Well, no wonder he did not protect your dog (who had been run over by a car); you are talking to a dead man!" Now looking back, I can see how heartless that must have sounded to him, but he was used to our banter back and forth about our beliefs.

Another time he had invited my then-husband and me to a St Patrick's Day dinner at the Catholic Church. We were surprised to see that they served beer right inside the church! I believe ex-hubby asked at that point if we could switch religions.

At his funeral, I watched as they prayed the rosary. I had never witnessed such a thing and at some point, I felt him standing next to me. At first, I thought I was imagining it, but I began a conversation with him in my head anyway, just in case. I told him that he had a lot of friends and family, and he must feel good that so many people showed up to say goodbye. I also remarked on the length of the rosary ceremony, just because was typical of our relationship to question each other's religious practices.

Years later a fellow medium asked me, "Who is Joe?" I remarked that the only Joe I knew was my good friend from work who had passed years before. She said he wanted to say thank you; I had helped him cross over. That made me feel good because I didn't know I had helped. Our conversation at the funeral was real. I felt that it was but at the time, it didn't fit into my belief system.

The Nurse at the Funeral

On another occasion I was attending a funeral with my current husband. We were both somewhat acquainted with the family, but I had limited knowledge of the details of the deceased's past. She had suffered from dementia and although we had met several times and even spent some time together, she did not remember me.

At first, before the funeral actually started, I saw a nurse walk by in one of those old-fashioned white nurse's dresses and even the nurse's cap they used to wear. I did not realize at first it was the deceased. I remember wondering, *Who is the nurse?* Sometimes the dead present themselves in a time period in which they were most happy, or when a significant emotional event had occurred. Not realizing that the nurse was the deceased to whom we were paying our respects, I had tuned in to her and started a conversation. One of those, "Hi, what is your name and why are you here?" kind of conversations. At first, she did not directly communicate with me but I sensed that she had spent some time as a nurse either in the military or in some way related to soldiers. She told me she had been in love with a soldier in her younger days. The soldier and she had never worked out. I was not sure if he had died or what had happened, but I got a sense that in some way he had left and they had never been able to be together. Then she vanished.

A few minutes later I saw her appear as her older self. She looked at me and acted a bit confused. She asked me who I was and was not even a little bit friendly to me. In life she was not afraid to speak her mind and I imagine this would have been an appropriate response due to the dynamics of my relationship to the family.

I told Clay of my experiences but I was hesitant to tell the family members. Later, at the house where family members gathered, I asked one of the relatives to share a bit about her past. One of the woman's daughters revealed that her mother had been a nurse during war times and before she met and married her father, she had been in love with a soldier.

In the beginning stages of developing my gift, I used to practice a lot on family and friends and one of my regular "practice" friends told me that the message I gave her from her mother was the first time anyone had been able to connect with her and the message had indeed brought some healing to their relationship. I also found that at times, when I began to offer my services of connecting to Spirit and delivering messages, clients would not be interested in messages from their Guides or information about their life or future. What they really wanted was to talk to their dead son or brother. I was not at all confident in my abilities at first and used to agree to attempt to talk to them with a disclaimer that it was really not my specialty.

I Can't Do This!

When I booked a client who specifically told me that she wanted to talk to her brother and I had conveyed to her my disclaimer, Spirit came to me the morning of the reading and chided me just a bit. Spirit is always gentle and yet firm with their corrections. My Guides told me that it was my own doubts that were blocking the reception. They instructed me to proclaim all day long, "I am an amazing medium and I will connect successfully with this person!"

Needless to say, the affirmations worked and the client's brother came through with amazing accuracy. I was able to describe her brother's personality and his state of mind at the time of his death. He also gave his sister a message about the suspicious circumstances of his death.

Remember that when people pass, they will come back to communicate in a similar fashion as they would if they were still with us. They do not cross over to the other side and immediately become enlightened.

Mary's Dirty Laundry

Once I was conducting a spirit circle and one of the participants asked about a woman named Mary. I immediately saw clothesline and clothes hanging on the line. After determining that the clothesline had no particular meaning, I exclaimed, "Oh, but did she have some dirty laundry?" The clothesline ended up being symbolic for the way she lived her life. This turned out to be the case.

When the participants were convinced I had Mary, one of them asked, "What does she have to say about Frank?" Immediately I heard, "That son of a bitch!" When I asked the participants what that meant, one of them proclaimed that Frank was the man who killed her!

I am happy that I did not doubt the information that came through or decide to water down what she said. Sometimes you just have to relay the information word for word, no matter how inappropriate it seems. However, some sensitive information may have to be communicated delicately.

Once again, doubt cuts off the ability to connect with Spirit, whether it is an Angel, a Guide, a dead relative, or even a pet. Believing that Spirit wants to connect and believing in the connection itself is the key that opens the door. Most mediums will agree that it is fairly difficult to connect with your own family on the other side, but they do occasionally show up with a message or a sign of their presence.

Clay's Mother

When my youngest granddaughter was born, we had an electric swing in the living room which we often used when she was there. On more than one occasion, her great-grandmother, Clay's mother, made her presence known when she was at our home. One time I was alone in the house with my granddaughter and she had fallen asleep in her swing. I left her in the swing and went into the other room to do some work. Clay's mother showed up, insisting I go out to where my granddaughter was. I guess she thought I had left her in the room by herself for quite long enough. On another occasion, I was in the room with a friend and the swing began going back and forth on its own with no involvement on my part. Reagan was not even there at the time but apparently Clay's mother was there and wanted to show herself.

Eventually I created what I affectionately call an ancestor altar, containing items that belonged to both Clay's deceased family members and mine. We found that no matter what room we chose to house the ancestor altar in, it was the room with the most noises, knocks, and creaks. Apparently, the altar has the tendency to draw their energy into whatever room it is housed.

When the dead come through, I always ask them to give me information that may not necessarily be important but will, without question, convince their loved ones that the information is in fact, coming from them. I had a client's cousin come through showing me a manhole. The client immediately knew it was her cousin because as children they used to play in manholes. A mother came through showing her daughter her favorite color of lipstick and her affection for nice clothes and jewelry. One recent mother came through showing me pink flowers. That very morning her daughter, my client, had bought some pink carnations in honor of her mother. Pink carnations were her favorite!

One client's mother showed me an old-fashioned broom. I made the mistake of trying to get the symbolism of a broom, maybe representing sweeping something under the table so to speak, but my client explained that no, her mother had given her one of those decorative brooms with potpourri that you hang on your door.

What Happened to Your Pearls?

Recently I worked with a client who wished to communicate with her grandmother. Immediately I saw a woman wearing nice clothes and a matching hat. She had curls coming out from under the hat. She was wearing a pearl necklace and matching earrings. The client instantly knew it was her grandmother because one of the questions she had for her was, "Whatever happened to your pearl necklace and earrings you promised me?"

Continuing on, I saw that she loved nice things. I saw a silver platter, a teapot, and perhaps silver teaspoons. I saw crocheted doilies on the tables. But I noticed a lack of people. No children running about. The house seemed empty. I did see a large dictionary that I felt represented words, communication, and education. My client agreed and revealed that her grandmother was the only one in her family who had graduated college, a fact of which she was proud.

The client agreed that she valued nice things more than family. The client actually had received one of her grandmother's teapots and related that she crocheted the doilies herself. She asked her grandmother if her first husband, my client's grandfather was around. I saw a nicely dressed man in a library.

The library ended up being a reference to the client's occupation as a historian and her love of words. My client asked if he minded that her grandmother had been buried next to him, despite having left him in life. He confessed that the divorce was her idea, not his, and that he loved her to the day he died, which my client confirmed. I sensed that the woman could not have imagined being married to only one man for her whole life and that she loved adventure and new experiences, finding marriage and children somewhat boring. The client then revealed that her grandmother had left her husband and seven children to marry another man, the second of three husbands.

People ask me if the dead wake me up at night or if I see the dead walking around like some of those shows on television. I have had the occasional experience of being woken up by spirits, but it is not something that happens regularly. Spirit normally will show me inner visions, or play a song in my head over and over, or I will just "know."

Off the Deep End

Recently the father of a good friend passed away. I was awakened in the wee hours of the morning the day after his passing. The words of a song were running through my head: "I'm on the deep end, watch as I dive in...." I felt a sense of joy as my friend's father headed toward the light. I felt as if he was swimming to the light, and that his guides were dolphins. I really didn't know anything about him, despite knowing his daughter. I had met him once, briefly, at a party, so I didn't have any pre-conceived notions of what his life was like or if he even liked swimming or dolphins.

Obviously at three in the morning I was hesitant to text my friend with the message from her father. I told him I would text her later in the morning, but he was fairly insistent that I do it at that moment. He was probably worried I would forget, which was a distinct possibility.

I went ahead and texted her the message from her father, and then I was able to go back to sleep. Thankfully she must have turned her phone off because there was no immediate response. Later that morning she texted me back. The reference to swimming or dolphins was not immediately recognizable to her, but my friend reported that her father's lungs were filled with fluid at the time of his death. Maybe in some way that fluid was giving him the feeling of swimming.

The Lost Broach

Sometimes clients come in to see me feeling more than a little bit skeptical. That is fine, but I do sometimes have more difficulty tuning in to those who are questioning the information. I recently learned that the father of one of my regular clients was one of those people. Hannah was a frequent client, who began bringing her family members to see me on various occasions. At one point she came to see me in the company of her father.

I knew that he was not overly impressed with the information that came through and maybe even a little disappointed.

During the session with Hannah and her dad, I mentioned a family brooch. I saw that it was missing and that there were family members researching its disappearance. Hannah's father admitted that he did not know anything about the piece of jewelry and found it doubtful that anyone was looking for it.

A few days later, Hannah's father showed up in her kitchen carrying a large book containing papers and clippings of family information. He opened the book to a specific page and slammed it down in front of his daughter. On the page was a correspondence of some kind with a photo of a family brooch-and queries into its whereabouts.

Little things sometimes become catalysts to make believers out of skeptics. I guess he is a believer now.

CHAPTER EIGHT

SOUL HEALINGS

Healing of the soul has been around for a long time, though it is sometimes labeled differently. When I was going to church it was called "inner healing." In shamanism it is called "soul retrieval." This is the term that originally sparked my interest in the type of soul healing that I do.

I first learned the term *soul retrieval* many years ago when my husband started attending spirit circles with medium Terri Rodabaugh. At one particular circle we attended, we took my stepdaughter along, who was fairly young at the time. Terri would go around the circle and connect with dead friends and relatives and Spirit Guides to bring each participant a message from the spirit world. During this particular circle, Terri suggested that my stepdaughter could benefit from a soul retrieval. She explained that normally soul retrievals are performed by a shaman. I was intrigued.

After the circle, I went home and ordered five books on shamanism and soul retrievals. We also searched for a shaman but found that there were none close by, at least that advertised on the internet. About halfway through the first book, I had what I guess would be a spontaneous past-life memory or an 'aha' moment. I knew without a doubt that I had done soul retrievals before but not in this life, and not only that, I knew how to do them.

Ecstatic at this discovery, I jumped up and ran inside to give Clay the good news. Honestly, I was not really sure how he would react. Only recently had I revealed to him that I could hear Spirit talking to me and that I have had the gift a long time. Now I was going to tell him that I thought I may have been a shaman in a previous life and I thought I knew how to do soul retrievals. I should not have been surprised that he was completely supportive and encouraged me to try to find a teacher or whatever I needed to do.

At first, I had no success finding a teacher or classes in the area that fit into my budget and worked around my day job. I was not deterred from my determination. I began to call on friends and family to allow me to do "journeys" for them (another shamanic term for the altered state of consciousness one goes into to perform this healing). For about three years I practiced on family and friends. Eventually some friends of friends began to contact me as well as acquaintances, or people who somehow found out about me. Another medium, Susan Lynne, began to call on me to help with some of her clients. Mostly I was doing the healings for free or a very small fee. I had not had any formal training and was not comfortable charging the rates I saw other shamans charging.

Looking back, I feel that it turned out to be a good thing that I was listening to Spirit and performing the healings with only the guidance of my guides and the instructions I had read in the books. When I finally took some classes, some of the techniques I had been using were discouraged or forbidden. However, I have learned to trust my Guides, and I had gotten good results using the techniques they taught me.

So exactly what is a soul healing or a soul retrieval?

I mentioned in a previous chapter that many times what is often mistaken for a ghost, is actually trapped emotions that have gotten imprinted in a particular location. In those times when you experience trauma or an extremely emotional event, pieces of yourself, whether you call it your soul, your emotional body, your essence or your energy field, get separated from your physical body. These pieces can get trapped in physical locations or somewhere in the non-physical realm. We also sometimes lose pieces of ourselves to other people.

When I do a soul healing, I enter an altered state of consciousness through drumming, rattling, or other repetitive music, or even with no sound at all, and Spirit takes me to where the soul pieces are hiding. I can also retrieve them from other people, places, or time periods. Many people find extreme changes in their lives after a soul retrieval.

Soni's Story

Here is one story from a friend and colleague, Soni Weiss, Ph.D., CH:

Over the years, as a student of metaphysics, I had read about and talked with several people who had experienced soul retrieval, so when I met Joy and learned she did this work I was quick to book a session with her.

As soon as I entered the front door, I could feel a change in the energy. Joy escorted my friend (who had booked a session also) and me to the living room of her home where she proceeded to explain to us how the session would progress. As Joy talked to us, I felt a strong current of air come through the closed and draped windows carrying what seemed to be leaf like objects with it. My friend was asking questions and listening to Joy, neither of whom seemed to notice the gust of wind. I thought, okay, Soni, this should be really interesting afternoon, and I was proven right.

When it was time for my session to start, Joy had me lie down on her table and told me she would begin the session using her new drum which she had some doubts about. I really disliked Indian drums and could never understand why anyone would go to a drumming session for pleasure let alone healing, as all they ever did was irritate the heck out of me. Well, I was here and it was her table and the noise can't last forever I thought. As Joy began beating the drum, I closed my eyes and let my mind wander, mainly to distract me from the sound of the drum, and it took me to a cabin in an isolated farm area. I knew there was no one around for miles and miles. I was in the cabin with my two children, all huddled together and very afraid. As I observed the event in my mind, I realized how totally alone and isolated we had always been and how depressed and unhappy I was with this life that had no hope of ever changing. Then I heard the drumming and I understood we were surrounded by Indians whose land we had taken to use as farmland. They wanted their land back and they were setting the cabin on fire. We eventually would die in the fire. I realized that although there were weapons in the cabin, I made no attempt to fight or run, and I passively allowed us all to die.

Being a past-life regressionist, I immediately connected this event to things that have happened in my current life. I could see patterns in these events and was grateful for the insights this soul retrieval gave me regarding numerous issues I had been trying to figure out. Not liking the sound of the drums certainly made sense now. From that point on, the sound of the drums has not bothered me at all. Doors were opening and continued to open throughout the session.

Toward the end of the session Joy asked me if I knew someone who had a broken leg. Someone with a cast on their leg was hanging onto my ankle with a strong grip and she had to really work to pry them loose. At first, I said no, then I realized who it was. She didn't have a cast though. She had a walking boot on, as she had recently been hit by a car in the parking lot at work. Joy released her and we did some forgiveness work clearing our relationships from the past and present. The individual was in a position to have a significant impact on my life and our relationship changed after the session. The woman totally left my life within a year.

I noticed positive changes over the next few months after the session. One was that empty place in my abdomen didn't seem so large anymore. It had shrunk considerably as I learned how to call back my little bits of energy left with others as our lives interact, and returned others' energy so as not to be weighed down by theirs left with me.

Here are some common questions I often hear when explaining the process.

"Do I have to come to you in person or can you do it long distance?"

Before my formal training, I did perform soul retrievals long distance and I still do. After several years, I decided to take a class just to see if I was on the same page as the traditional shaman. My teacher told me that it was impossible to do a soul retrieval long distance. *Hmm. I am sure I was successful performing them and the people had responded positively.*

My mentor Susan Lynne had a client on the other side of the country who had a relative in the hospital who had suffered a stroke. The patient's wife was inconsolable. She had been in the hospital at his bedside for two weeks without going home to shower or eat. Susan asked if I could help.

I contacted his soul remotely and found him in that in-between place. There was a tunnel of light made up of a beautiful array of colors. His soul was in the tunnel but was torn between staying and moving on. I also saw him and his wife doing ballroom dancing. I knew that his concern was for his wife. He wanted to go but felt a connection and responsibility for her grief. I talked to his soul but did not tell him he had to return to his body. I gave him permission to do whatever was best for his soul.

When Susan related what I saw, the client mentioned that they had met while ballroom dancing and it was their favorite pastime. At around the time that I connected to his soul, he woke up, sat up in bed and talked to his wife a bit. The next day he passed.

On another occasion a client of Susan's came to her regarding a son who had been missing for a period of time. I connected with the son's soul, found some missing pieces, and told him his parents were worried. I told Susan he was living in California in a small apartment. A few days later he reconnected with his parents. Which leads to the next question.

"Can you perform a soul retrieval on someone without their knowledge or permission?"

I can go into an altered state and ask the person's soul for permission. Most of the time their soul says, "yes," but sometimes they do not give permission. If they want to talk, I can communicate with their soul. Their conscious mind will most likely not remember the communication but their actions may shift. Just as the boy who was reconnected with his parents when I told him they were worried about him, there may be an action needed that they wake up and decide to take. And sometimes not. Remember that free will is one of the rules of the universe. As I mentioned before, normally this question comes from mothers asking about healing their children.

"Are soul pieces ever recovered from the future before something even happens?"

In the beginning, I performed a soul retrieval for a long-distance client. I related to her the pieces I found and put back into her body remotely. I am usually given some kind of visual of what I see and where the pieces are located, which I shared with her in a letter.

Being polite, she never shared with me that the communication never rang true at the time. However, several years later she told me that she had found the letter sometime after, and even though the soul retrieval had happened several years before, the events I described had just happened to her in the past year. She completely understood each scenario I had described. Spirit gave her back her soul pieces before she even lost them! Remember that time and space only exist in our world, not in the spirit world, so it is just as easy to recover soul pieces from the future as from the past.

Here is how she relates the story:

Priscilla's Story

I first met Joy at a book signing in Frederick MD. While we chatted, she informed me that I could get a soul retrieval to go on her web site. It piqued my curiosity so I emailed Joy. Joy responded and asked that I send something personal. At the time, I was just learning about the metaphysical world of crystals. Rose quartz is one of my power stones because of its energy of love. Without thinking I dropped it in a plain envelope and sent it off.

A week later Joy sent another email saying that she was finished with the soul retrieval. I asked her to send it in the mail because I didn't want my husband freaking out. He isn't a believer.

When I got the letter, it spoke of visions of wine glasses and flowers with smoke in the air. There was much more to the visions. Joy also witnessed my fox animal totem playing in a field. I thought, Wow. How did she know that? I just had a Reiki master reveal that the fox energy was part of me. I thought of what the visions meant for me and didn't think much more about them.

Later in the month my entire self-image and belief system crashed. I guess you could say it was a mid-life crisis. I put myself first instead of my family and worst of all, I thought I was entitled to more. My whole thought process shifted. I drank every day and started smoking. It was like a poison running through my veins. I started going out whenever I had the chance. I avoided being a wife and mom. It was a rough 6 months. The bough broke the day after Thanksgiving and I thought for sure that my husband was going to leave me.

Three times throughout my chaotic mess I saw a real fox; twice while driving and one that crossed in front of me in my driveway. I associated the fox with being elusive and beautiful. Several years later, that association changed. The fox was now revealing warnings and deceptions. My husband told me I had to stop drinking, and I did; for three months. However, I still had the urge to be so-called, free. Honestly that part of me took a couple years to return back to center. It wasn't the drinking that haunted me, it was the shift in my thought *process; the idea that I work hard and I deserve more than what God has provided me.*

I went to Joy for a healing session after my downward spiral. Looking directly into my heart she saw three arrows jammed in it. Joy told me that she had to pull them out of there because they were blocking my healing process. These arrows were negative energy and symbols of what my ego was clinging to. I never felt so much pain! Each arrow was extremely, physically painful. I was yelling with each pull. I thought that her husband, Clay, was going to come in the room. I had no idea that I was so blocked. I felt relieved when Joy's hands gently held me. She gave me instructions to talk to my heart every day and say, "Little one, it will be okay. You are loved."

Interestingly, the soul retrieval was set for my future, not the present time when Joy was working with my spirit. The visions of wine glasses and smoke rising in flowers were pieces of my soul lost to my shift in thought. Joy witnessed what was going to happen in a symbolic way. As always, spirit works in mysterious ways. Accept the unexpected.

Clarity has returned to my life. It took such a long time for my higher self to come forth. I am so grateful for my husband and children's love and patience. I look for opportunities to share my wisdom that I gained from this difficult lesson with others. I am open to others when they are faced with challenges. In the end I became a better wife, mom and friend. When the fox comes to me now, I know to look for warnings and deceptions. The fox helps me avoid the pitfalls of negative energy.

"Do animals lose pieces of their souls?"

I do believe that animals, like people, often experience trauma and certainly can lose pieces of their souls. I have done soul healings on animals and sometimes it does aid them in processing difficult experiences.

That being said, there is a difference between a lost soul and the cords of energy that tie us to people, places, animals, and things. When we think about a person or an animal, or even a location, and accompany those thoughts with intense emotions like grief, sadness, anger, or even love, cords of energy are created between us and the subjects of our obsessions. This is different from soul loss but can mirror the symptoms.

Probably as often as I connect with loved ones on the other side, I connect with beloved pets who are attached to my clients through the affection that they shared. On at least one occasion the pet was unable to cross to the other side due to the owner's intense grief.

It is extremely important to release our loved ones and pets from the emotion of grief so that they can safely make it to the other side and move on to the next expression of their soul. Dogs especially, seem to incarnate with the sole purpose of serving their people. So, when a person grieves significantly, the cord becomes too strong for the animal to penetrate. The animal feels the strong emotions of the person with whom they were in a relationship in life, and many times even feels the emotions the living feel. If there is a significant bond, the pet will stick around in the in-between place, not able to communicate or show affection to its person but feeling his or her emotions. It is so important to get through the grieving process and allow your pet to cross over. Obviously, this is also true for our human loved ones.

"Can you be missing a soul piece from another lifetime?"

My shamanic mentor taught me that when a person dies, they take with them all of their issues from the current lifetime to be processed. Thus, soul retrievals should never cross over to other lifetimes. However, I have not always found this to be the case. I have found many soul pieces in other lifetimes and the location of the soul piece often mirrored a current life issue or experience.

I had one client for whom I found a soul piece up in a tree. She had been a soldier in another lifetime, and when she passed in that lifetime, her soul had remained in the physical location up in a tree. When I recounted to her the story of the soul piece up in a tree, she told me that once as a child she had run away from home and had climbed a tree where she remained for three days. I was able to retrieve both the piece of her soul left in the tree from the other lifetime as a soldier, and the one that she had left there as a child. Trauma is trauma and our souls remember, whether it happened in this incarnation or another.

Many times, healing comes from simply reminding our souls that we are in this particular life experience, and release the soul memories in the cells of our bodies.

"Can someone who has passed have a piece of my soul?"

Yes! Either you could have given it to them or they could have stolen it but many times in healing sessions I am able to retrieve soul pieces from people on the other side. Then there is the related healing technique of cutting the energetic cords that exist between us and other people. Those people can be living or dead. These two techniques can happen in one session or over the course of a series of sessions.

"What is the process for retrieving the soul pieces?"

Every session I have with a client will be different. I am completely led by my Spirit Guides in the process. I have no set expectations for how a session will unfold. Many shamanic practitioners have a format that they adhere to when going into the non-physical worlds. My sessions are a bit different. Sometimes I follow the format and sometimes I don't. Sometimes I don't know I am going to do a soul retrieval until I get into the session with the client. Sometimes I retrieve the soul pieces and then recount the stories of the soul pieces before placing them back into the body of the client. There are times when I lead them into a light-altered state of consciousness and they are able to get their soul pieces back themselves. This is always done with the presence and participation of my Benevolent Helpers and the Helpers of the clients. Either way, healing comes.

Recently I worked with a client who had suffered from a string of failed relationships. We had been working together for quite some time over this pattern, but it seemed to continue, despite the work that we had done.

In preparation for her visit on one particular occasion, I was told in meditation to do a session in which the client would exchange soul pieces with past lovers. We had done this on a previous visit, but I decided that if Spirit wanted us to do it again, we would follow Spirit's instructions.

I found that one of the past relationships involved a man who was very controlled by his mother, which the client confirmed. I believed that the mother was trying to reignite the relationship and was unconsciously or consciously doing some sort of manipulation of energy to reconnect her son to my client.

Using remote viewing, I went into her house and asked my client if the mother had a decorative box of some sort that had belonged to her. She confirmed that she had given it to her as a gift. I had to extract my client's essence from this and any other items that had belonged to her to prevent any manipulation of energy causing distress to my client. My client confirmed she had felt a dark presence lately in her home and felt it was related to this past lover, as sometimes she would awaken and feel his presence. I conversed with the mother's soul and asked her to desist from whatever she was doing. It was important to allow her son to make his own choices, despite her feelings that he was making a mistake. I also requested that she cease her activities involving my client.

In this case, I worked with my client's higher self and her combined intuitive ability with mine, to retrieve the energy that was missing in her physical body. When I retrieved the soul pieces, I asked her higher self to heal the soul pieces before returning them to her body. After the session, the client later reported that she had gone home and slept for almost four hours. She had felt a release and a complete change in her energy.

Yes, at this point in my life, I do believe it is possible to manipulate someone's energy without their permission, as I felt this ex-lover's mother was doing. She may have been doing it consciously or unconsciously, but her intentions, or prayers, or whatever she was doing, were having an ill-effect on my client. These are things I cannot know until I go into an altered state of consciousness during my sessions with clients. My Higher Guidance System gives me the information and then tells me what to do to correct the situation.

I would like to stress though, that these healings can be undone through the choices of the client. If I heal a piece of a client's soul that was lost or damaged due to a toxic relationship but the client continues in the relationship, the healing will be short-lived. Soul healing, many times, is like peeling the layers of an onion. One healing session is often not enough to reverse years of trauma or repetitive disempowering behavior.

There is also the possibility that the client is in some way benefitting from the toxic behavior. They think they want healing, but when faced with the possibility of having to live without the toxic person or behavior, they revert back to the toxic behavior. Soul healings are a collaboration between the healer and the client. A client has to be committed to their healing. They have to be committed to changing their behavior once the healing is complete.

This is not a miracle procedure. Healing of the soul is a process. It is kind of like losing weight. An overweight person can diet and exercise for a while and lose weight but if the everyday behavior is not consistent, the weight will come back. Weight issues by the way, can also stem from emotional issues that can sometimes be corrected with soul healings. But eating is a habit and once the healing occurs, the habit of eating badly or not exercising has to be reversed.

One healing practice is that of talking to the souls of people with whom you have not experienced closure. This is done by going into a state of meditation or a light trance and imagining the person is standing in front of you. You are actually connecting with that person's soul or essence. Although the conscious awareness of that person will probably not acknowledge the communication, on a soul level the person will hear you. Spirit told me years ago that the best way to do this is to wait until the person is asleep, but I have found that is not always necessary. The important part is the communication itself. Tell the person what you may not be able to tell them if they were actually standing in front of you. Tell them the down and dirty truth of how you really feel—not how you think you are supposed to feel, or how an enlightened or spiritually aware person should feel. Just let it all out.

Then forgive.

Forgive yourself for your part in the relationship, and forgive the other person for their part. At some level, there was a soul agreement,

before birth perhaps or in another place and time, when you both agreed to the experience.

Then let it go.

Sometimes, miraculously, the person with whom you communicate receives the message and acknowledges, or in some way receives the communication. But more importantly, you are changed. You have let go of the poison inside and admitted to yourself the truth of how you feel.

Jesus Gave Me My Soul Back

Years after I left the church and thought that all of my wounds had healed, Jesus came to me while I was running. He told me that he had a piece of my soul that he wanted to return. I was astounded! Of course, one of the tenets of our faith was that of giving one's heart and soul to Jesus. I had done it numerous times, fearing that the first time didn't take. I was more than a little surprised that Jesus wanted to give me back my soul.

I probably argued with him a little. "Don't you think you should keep it?" I asked him. "After all, you are Jesus."

"No, Joy," He said to me. "You need all of your soul pieces to be whole, including the ones you gave me. You will be fine." So, Jesus gave me back my soul.

The first couple days after receiving my soul back from Jesus, I was mad. I was mad at everyone. I lost my temper with the other drivers around me on the road, the customers at work over the tiniest little infraction from anyone who came into my presence. After three days of this, I began to wonder why I was so mad. I realized that my soul had been really mad when I left the church and I had been secretly mad at Jesus too. The soul piece that Jesus gave back to me was a very angry piece of myself.

I had a conversation with my recovered soul piece and told her that everything was okay now. I had really learned a lot from the experience and was surprisingly happy that the whole incident had occurred. I had found my truth and empowered myself. I had embraced my gift and had learned (or remembered) a lot of new truth of which I was previously unaware.

After bringing my recovered soul piece into present time and assuring her that all was well, the anger subsided. I was able to feel joy again and let go of all the anger from my years of stuffing down those emotions. After all, who would admit they were mad at Jesus?

I did learn a lot from this interaction with Jesus. Previously, I had not understood the importance of healing the soul pieces that I recovered before putting them back into my clients' bodies. Now, I always run the soul pieces through an Angel, a deity, or the client's highest self, or I hold the soul piece and send it Reiki before inserting it back into the bodies of my clients. I always tell people that there is no general rule on what to expect when you get a soul piece back. Some people will feel joy, some will get sick for a day or two, and some will find the need to sleep more than usual. The key is to be gentle with yourself and notice any shifts in awareness or any conflicting emotions. After four or five days, the soul piece normally adjusts.

Remember, that piece of your soul has been absent from your body for a period of time. There is a natural adjustment period. It helps to communicate with that soul piece and express your love and appreciation with it for coming back to you.

CHAPTER NINE

MEDIUM ON THE SIDE

As of the writing of this book, I just recently retired from my day job, where I had been for thirty-one years. In my chapter on rituals, I tell the story of how I was able to manifest a position at a particular location closer to my home and a particular position within the company.

So many of my clients tell me they would love to quit their jobs and make a living doing their spiritual work. Although for years I dreamed of making my living from giving messages from the Spirit world, I also like to eat and pay my bills on time. There are many people who are able to make a living doing readings and healings, etc., but there are many who try and fail. I chose for most of my adult life to be a messenger on the side for Spirit, while allowing the day job to pay me.

So, what happens when my two worlds collide? I credit the day job with affording me the opportunity to begin to receive messages from Spirit again, even before I had gone through my "dark night of the soul" when I turned off my gift.

In the church my first husband and I attended, receiving messages from the Holy Spirit was an integral part of the soul of the church. I was given the opportunity to deliver messages with the full blessing and even nurturing of the pastors. During that time, I worked nights, (so I guess you could actually term it my "night job") and spent hours doing mindless repetitive work. While other employees would listen to music on headphones, I was receiving information and wisdom from Source under the umbrella of that faith. It was during this time that I began to receive information which was not completely in line with the belief system in which I was involved.

In one moment of a download from the Spirit world while I was working, my whole world came crashing down. I did not know who I was or why I was here. I did not know the meaning of life.

If these things I have believed all of my life
aren't true, then my whole life is a lie.

Around that time, I had taken my daughter to see a Disney film in which a toy realizes he is, in reality, a toy, and not a superhero. The toy is devastated and loses all of his will to live or carry on. I knew exactly how he felt!! All of my beliefs about God, Jesus, life, death, and my purpose in life came up for review.

This was the beginning of my dark night of the soul. And it all started from working nights while the rest of the world slept.

Thankfully, not all of the messages I received at work were as life-changing for me. Some of them, however, were life-changing for other people.

A Fish on a Hook

Because my coworkers did not always share my beliefs, I had to learn to formulate a method of delivering the words of wisdom without them realizing I was giving them a message from Spirit. On one occasion I predicted an event in which a coworker was on vacation and fell off a boat with his foot tied to the anchor of the boat. My exact words had been: "God has you like a fish on a hook and is reeling you in." He was, in fact, reeled in just like a fish with his foot tied up in the rope that is tied to the anchor which some would say resembles a hook. It took me some time to learn to express the visions I saw in a way that did not reflect my faith.

After my departure from the church, the messages stopped for several years. I attributed this lack of communication to the anger I felt toward God and His purported messengers misleading me by telling me things that were not true. I was also mad that the messages I received from Spirit were getting me in trouble and causing me to be ousted from what I considered to be my purpose in life as a spirit messenger. I could not imagine myself without the church. I had no concept of a way to deliver messages without that platform. Eventually, years later, after I once again started receiving and delivering messages, I tried to keep my two worlds separate, but that didn't always work.

I am forbidden by the ethics regulations at the Post Office which employed me for thirty-one years from using my position there to generate business for any other occupation, which includes soliciting clients while on the job. Conducting client readings while working would obviously be a no-no. I can say I never received payment for any messages I received or delivered while on the job. However, I have a couple of cool stories of what happens when the world of career and the world of Spirit collide.

My colleagues at the day job were not all aware of what I was doing "on the side," but word sometimes got around.

The Lost Baby

One day I was minding my own business, doing my thing, when one of my coworkers approached me. She had been struggling with some stomach pain. She had been to the doctors, had tests done, and came up empty. I knew of her struggle but had offered no assistance. I feel it was unethical to offer help if I wasn't asked. My friend approached me that day and made no attempt to hide her dismay.

"Joy, when are you going to help me?" was her unexpected question.

I explained that I never help unless asked.

"Well I am asking."

I agreed to *tune in* on my lunch break and see what, if anything, I came up with. I never promise to deliver a miracle cure for any illness, but many times I am able to pinpoint an emotional trigger to an illness, especially if it is undiagnosed despite multiple tests and trips to the doctor. If an emotional trigger is discovered, often an unexplained illness or pain can be eliminated by dealing with the emotional trigger.

While on break, I was given the answer. I told my colleague that she would have to come to my house after hours to hear what I had garnered, and for me to help her, which she readily agreed to do. We made a plan for her to come by after work one day and she promptly showed up as scheduled. I revealed to her that I had talked to the child she had lost more than twenty years before. I do not remember ever knowing beforehand that she had lost a child, but she confirmed that she had delivered a stillborn baby. I asked her if she still felt guilt over the loss or grieved for the lost child. She began to weep.

The message I received from the stillborn child was that it was not her fault. She had done nothing wrong and there was no reason to feel shame or guilt. The child also revealed that one of her grandchildren actually carried the essence of that child's energy. I would say that the soul of the stillborn child had reincarnated as one of her grandchildren. For those who are not quite on board with reincarnation, I will word it to say that one of the grandchildren had a special bond with this woman and that is the one who carried at least a portion of the stillborn child's essence.

Immediately my colleague knew which one it was and confirmed that, yes, she had a special bond with one of her grandchildren, although she loved them all. She went home, leaving behind a ton of tears and the pain in her abdomen. Several years later, she confirmed that the physical pain she had experienced prior to our session had never returned.

I know the question some of you may have: If a soul has reincarnated, how am I able to talk with them? Remember, I talk to the soul and souls transcend time and space. They are eternal. The soul has the memory of every lifetime and can talk about any one of them. Our conscious minds are not our souls and most of the time do not remember all that information. It would drive us crazy!

I have talked to the souls of people both living and dead. I sometimes give messages to people from loved ones who are still in their bodies. I will admit that sometimes it is hard to tell. Those souls start talking and I don't always ask them if they are in their bodies or not. Remember I am just the messenger. In a previous chapter on what happens when we die, I related the wisdom of one of my Guides who said that we are all like droplets of water in an ocean. We are all part of a whole, and we are also all part of one another. By tuning in to the consciousness of one of the other drops of water in the ocean, I receive information and messages relevant to my clients, myself, and the world at large.

Message from Her Dog

One of my coworkers had lost her dog. She was frantic about finding her dog and came to me for help. At the time, I was meeting with a group of aspiring psychics and I took some items that belonged to the dog to my group and we all agreed that the dog had passed. Unfortunately, my coworker could not resolve herself to the loss. She grieved over the lost dog for a couple of years and would periodically come to me to ask me to reconnect and make sure that the dog was not just lost somewhere. Every time I got the same answer.

One day I was working at the front counter waiting on customers and my coworker stood in line and waited for me to wait on her. She was crying and wanted to know if I could just give her a message from her dog. Before I knew it, the dog came to me and told me that her grief was keeping him tied to her in the in-between world, preventing him from crossing over. It was very important to her dog's soul that she let him go. It was time. I told her she needed to have some sort of service for him and let him go to the other side.

Not to be repetitive, but this point bears repeating: Grief is a natural part of life. We all grieve the people, animals, and situations that we have loved to a certain degree. After a period of time, it is important to allow that person or animal to move on to the next expression of their soul. Grieving is for us. We feel the loss of that loved one in our lives. We may feel guilty replacing them in our lives. That is on us too. When we grieve for a very long time, our grief and our emotions tie us to the souls of our loved ones and neither are free to move on. At times it can bring their souls to a place of being attached to our energy fields. That is not healthy to either party. It is important to give our loved ones their freedom.

In the case of my coworker, our conversation happened at the front counter of the window while I was working. Sometimes you just have to throw caution to the wind and help people who are grieving, so I tried to talk quietly to her so as not to attract attention. I didn't want to get in trouble for giving a message from the other side while working. Most of the time, I tried to separate my job from my spiritual work, but sometimes Spirit has other ideas.

CHAPTER TEN

THE POWER OF RITUAL

We all believe in ritual whether we recognize it or not. Whether you watch your favorite sports event wearing a lucky jersey, or carry a rabbit's foot around with you, or maybe that quarter given to you by your grandfather, you have things that you believe help you in your day to day life.

I was first introduced to ritual while in a relationship with my version of Christianity. Baptism and communion are two of the best-known Christian rituals. Although we did not believe it in my version of Christianity, I understand that some believe that pouring water on one's head or being submerged in water actually changes a person physically, but most people who participate in this ritual believe that it assures them a place in Heaven. Depending on the sect of Christianity, the wine or juice in a communion service does not actually turn into the blood of Christ, but represents the participants' acknowledgement of their relationship with Jesus. The Bible and other religious and metaphysical texts are filled with various rituals which, when performed, change the circumstances of your life or shift the energy on a more universal scale.

Cleansing the Land of Bloodshed

I guess the first time I was exposed to or given a ritual which was out of the norm of the aforementioned ones, was from Spirit. It was to cleanse the land of the blood that had been shed on the property where my former church was located. This ritual was taken from a story in the Bible of the children of Israel when they marched around the walls of Jericho. Although now having knowledge about the consciousness of all things, and knowing that the blood itself has its own consciousness and connection to its host soul, and also knowing that the land itself contains its own version of consciousness, I would probably perform the ritual differently. At the time, Spirit used the information that I had based on my belief system to get the job done.

I led the participants who had agreed to help me in marching in circles on the land seven times. We danced and asked that the spirit of discontent and fighting amongst brothers be released. I don't remember if we had any noisemakers, but nowadays I would have used drums and rattles. I think Joshua, in the Bible, used trumpets. I do remember we danced and used our bodies and our words to release the energy.

Manifesting Change in Work Situations

On two occasions I was able to manifest change in my job situation using ritual. I had manifested a job at the Post Office due to a deal I made with Jesus where I had been working in a bar to pay the bills. I do believe in making deals, and in this case, I made the deal with Jesus. I had a husband with an inconsistent work ethic, so working the bar at the time was my best option. I had a young daughter and rent to pay. At one particular low point, I told Jesus that if he would get me a different job, I would go back to church and turn my life around. A week later I received an offer from the Post Office which would eventually employ me for the next thirty-one years. Given my subsequent experiences in the church, you may ask if, in retrospect, it ended up being a fair deal. Jesus got me out of the bar scene and my years in traditional Christianity gave me experiences

I would have never had in any other atmosphere, so, yes, I would say it was a fair deal, but...

But I had to commute an hour and a half each way to work. My daughter was three when I was hired. I was forced to leave her with babysitters, daycare, and ultimately my then-mother-in-law, while I worked. The guilt of leaving her for over twelve hours a day was too much for me, and my subconscious had created a recurring punishment for me. I was the victim of multiple car accidents. Some of them happened in my personal car and some with corporate vehicles, since my job description in the early years forced me to be on the road daily. I was in danger of being fired.

I knew there was a position within the Post Office which required no vehicle, and decided to look into it. I needed that position in order to continue my career because they were now hesitant to let me behind the wheel of their vehicles. My boss had also told me that because of my driving record, no other office would take me, so it would be a waste of time to apply for a transfer to a different office. I believed him so I never applied for a transfer anywhere else. Through my research into this alternative position, I found out the person who currently held the position was about to retire. However, positions were awarded according to seniority and I had none, so I worried my hopes would not be realized.

Frequently on the other employee's day off, though, management would let me fill the position to avoid having me in one of their vehicles. When I walked through my day while filling in for him, I would imagine energy going into the ground, and I would send out commands into the Universe that the position would be awarded to me. I imagined myself fulfilling the daily requirements of the job and that the position was mine. You guessed it. When my fellow employee retired, I was the only person who bid on that position and it was awarded to me. I happily maintained that position for over two years.

My then-husband shared my belief system and suggested we do a ritual to help me obtain a position in the town where I lived, and, hopefully, eliminate my three-hour round-trip commute every day. Why hadn't I thought of this before? We got in our car and drove around the local office three times and claimed a transfer opportunity for me in that location.

Nowadays, I pay attention to detail. If I were to do this ritual again, I would drive around the building clockwise, which is the direction of manifestation. I would go around three times on three consecutive days, and on the third day, I would drive around nine times. I did not know at the time that three is the number of manifestation and nine is the number of completion. I did the ritual according to the instructions I received, and it worked!

Spirit used the information that I had to manifest a position at my local office. I believe that details are important, but intention is the lighter fluid to any ritual. The natural thing I had to do was apply for a transfer. You can't expect Spirit to do everything! Within a week (YES, A WEEK!!) I had manifested a position in my local office.

Obtaining Citizenship

Recently one of my clients wanted a ritual to obtain citizenship. She had applied many months before and wanted some kind of indication that her application had been reviewed. We all know that these things take time, but I gave her a ritual to do nonetheless. I had her write on a piece of paper: *I now easily manifest citizenship in the United States*. I had her go onto the computer, find a picture of naturalization papers, print it out, and write her name on the paper in the appropriate spot.

For three days before the full moon, she danced clockwise around her papers and imagined herself as a U.S. citizen. The next time we talked, she told me that within a week she had received a letter from the U.S. government, approving her application for citizenship which she so desperately wanted. Was it the ritual or her intention that created the result? I say, both!

Creating what you want to manifest in your life can be as simple as deciding what you want, seeing yourself having it, and then creating a ritual to manifest it. You can use established symbols such as the directions, numbers, and phases of the moon. Or you can use whatever your belief system suggests. Some people enlist the assistance of their Higher Power. Whatever your belief system, the key is to see yourself with the object of your intention and then create a ritual for obtaining it. There are, however, some universal rules, or guidelines.

You should not do a ritual to make someone else do something.

It is not advisable to do a ritual to make someone fall in love with you. It is perfectly okay to do a ritual for love, but you should not have someone in particular in mind. I am not saying it cannot be done, but crossing free will is never advisable, and it creates karma you do not want to experience.

In my story of obtaining a particular position at work, I did not do the ritual until the person who had the position had already decided to retire. I do not want to do a ritual that is going to affect another person or animal negatively. Harm none. Remember the rule of three. Any ritual you do comes back on you three times. If you stick to doing rituals that are beneficial to everyone concerned, then your life can only get better.

I like the suggestion from Jesus in the Bible: *Do unto others what you would have others do to you.* When doing rituals, be specific, but leave wiggle room for adjustments.

Leave Spirit Some Wiggle Room!

Clay recently decided he would like to manifest a part-time job. He was specific in the hours he wanted to work, the days he wanted to work, and the salary he wanted to receive. After doing the ritual, he was searching online and found the kind of job he was looking for. He applied, had an interview, and was offered the position within just a few days.

Do Your Homework!

Remember that you still have to do your homework. You still have to apply for that job. For instance, you have to be somewhere or do something to meet the person of your dreams. Rarely do they just appear at your doorstep. (It could happen, but I would suggest you don't wait around for it.)

That being said, I don't feel you should have to pound the pavement and apply for a hundred different jobs. I am an advocate of being led in a particular direction. If you get a hunch that you should look at a website that offers jobs, then do it. If you are out driving around and a sign catches your eye for a particular company looking for employees, then maybe it is a sign that you should apply. Spirit can give you hints in a variety of ways. If an unusual ritual is presented to you and you feel drawn to do it, chances are you were drawn to that ritual for a reason. Do your research and give it a try!

Rule of Three

I was recently made aware that a person from my past was using his voice to spread negative information about me to people who were in both his circle of acquaintances and mine. I knew this was occurring but did not feel it was an issue. That is until my grandchildren began to approach me with questions about things that had happened with this individual before they were born.

I learned of a ritual that could be performed to cause him to cease his tongue-wagging. I must admit I was considering it, when one day I was talking to someone and the subject came up of people from our past. I recounted a few choice stories that reinforced my perspective of the situation. I have always held the viewpoint that when you perform a ritual, you should be aware of the rule of three. That is, any ritual you perform that will affect another person will affect you three times more. I immediately realized that if I did perform the ritual, I had to be willing to cease any and all gossip about him coming from me as well! Although most of the time I don't even think about him or hold him in any regard, positive or negative, there are times when a juicy story makes interesting conversation. No, this is probably not spiritually advisable, but we are all human! Who can say that they have never said a negative word about anyone?

As time went on, the person and I were put into a position of seeing one another at least on an occasional basis. I decided to speak kindly to him and acknowledge his presence when he was around. Although I can't say we are best buddies, we have found a place of peace. Had I done the ritual to tie his tongue, would this have occurred? I don't know.

Include items in your rituals that have meaning to you or symbolize things that are significant to you. If you are doing a ritual to manifest money, you might include a dollar bill or something that represents money or abundance to you. If you are doing a ritual to manifest love then you might want a heart, or flowers, or items that represent love. The ritual mentioned above that I had considered doing included a red velvet cut-out of a tongue. You get the idea.

Obtain Permission First!

Obviously, if you decide to do a ritual that involves obtaining items from specific locations, make sure you have permission from the owners or caretakers of the location. Always leave a gift or pay for the item you obtain in some way. Rituals don't work well if the items used have been stolen or obtained in a less than honorable way. Most of the time an intention, a candle, and instructions from the Universe as to the time and location of the ritual work just fine, but sometimes it is fun and beneficial to include items that represent what you are manifesting.

I recently heard about a ritual that uses dirt from seven graveyards. Although I have not taken the time to go to seven graveyards to obtain the dirt, and, frankly, I am not sure it is legal to take dirt from graveyards, the instructions specifically said you have to leave a gift in place of the dirt you take. Remember that everything you do is symbolic. Dirt, stones, water, and natural items you might obtain contain energy. Dirt from a graveyard might be thought to contain the energy or blessings from the person or type of person who is buried there.

It is thought that water from a thriving business contains the energy of prosperity. However, you can't just go into the bathroom of a bank and fill a bottle with water. You have to ask permission or pay for the water. Buying water in a thriving store might contain the energy of prosperity if the business is doing well and if the business does not thrive on the poverty of others. I would not get water for a ritual for prosperity, for example, from a discount store; not because it isn't a successful business, but for the fact that people shop there because it is cheap and affordable. I would rather obtain a bottle of water from a more prosperous, upscale establishment.

Respect Authority Figures

Sometimes ritual is not only for manifesting something you lack. Sometimes it is for spiritual renewal or inspiration. If you are participating in a ritual where someone else is in charge, you have to respect their rules.

Early on in my study of shamanism, I was invited to spend a weekend at the beach with some fellow shamanic students. We were instructed that for twenty-four hours before the ritual, we were not to drink any alcohol. This seems like a minor rule and most everyone was okay with it. Since leaving the church, I had developed a habit of drinking a glass of wine at night before bedtime. When faced with the challenge of giving up my nightly indulgence, I thought I was fine with it. I packed up my belongings for the weekend, and off I went to the beach, sans any wine or other comfort beverages. I might add that I was under the impression that the lack of alcohol was to ensure entry into ceremony being pure of body. I was mistaken.

When I arrived, the other participants had all brought snacks. I quickly ascertained that the snacks were in no way healthy. A huge chocolate cake adorned the kitchen table, and other snacks of every variety were open and available to all participants. Looking around, I noticed the person in charge outside was smoking cigarettes with about half of the other participants. I will admit I was more than a little bit stunned. That is when I realized that I *did* have a problem with leaving my wine at home. I do understand though, that tobacco is sacred to Native American traditions and alcohol has had a history of being a challenge to them. So, on some level, I understood but I didn't agree.

I also witnessed a good deal of cat fighting over the weekend. It is true that when you get a bunch of women together for a whole weekend, it is very likely that there will be misunderstandings or grievances. But it seemed to me the whole weekend was marred by an undercurrent of power struggles and petty disagreements, including my unspoken complaint about not having my glass of wine to take the edge off. I had spent the first thirty-five years of my life obeying rules that didn't make any sense, so I was keenly aware of the inconsistencies in this particular event. However, I was not in charge so I obeyed the rules. I did have some pretty amazing conversations with the seagulls that weekend and discovered, or remembered perhaps, an ability to talk to animals' souls as well as humans.

I left the event a little bit disgruntled, but this is what I learned: The person in charge makes the rules. If you don't like it, then do your own full moon event. Remember that sometimes the idea of a well-known ritual and what its benefits promise are sometimes more than the actual experience of it.

In subsequent years, I learned that this person completely changed her life by changing the foods she ate and the last full moon ritual was full of healthy snacks. I believe, though, that what you put in your body is not nearly as important as what you believe about it. Even Jesus said that what you put inside your body does not make you unclean. It is what comes out of you through your words, thoughts, and actions that make you unclean.

The experience I had was totally my interpretation and my issue. I realized that maybe my glass of wine was an issue and I have since addressed the habit. I still have a glass of wine on occasion, but I am not so focused on it that I allow the lack of it to ruin an experience.

If Someone Else Decides to Jump Off a Cliff...

As a student and practitioner of shamanism, you would think that I would enjoy participating in rituals such as a sweat lodge. I have one sweat lodge under my belt and unless my awareness or desires change, that would be enough for me. The idea is that when you are in a sweat lodge, you are sweating the toxicity out of your body and entering into an altered state of consciousness to bring spiritual experiences or enhanced awareness, or something of the sort. That was not my experience.

I had gone to participate in a weekend shamanic retreat at a mostly pagan parcel of land in Pennsylvania with a friend of mine. We went with expectations of revelations and shamanic experiences that would enhance our practices or our spiritual walks in some way or another.

It was April and the weather was cool. We quickly realized that it was also the rainy season. There were dorms for us to sleep in, but the showers were a good walk away and there was no hot water. We had not brought enough blankets or appropriate clothing to ward off the cold. Luckily there was no rule about drinking. In fact, one of the shamans had wine to sell, and it was not only allowed, but encouraged. He also sold drums, and I was able to purchase my now favorite drum. I have many hand-crafted, expensive drums that I bought from real, honest-to-goodness Native Americans, but they just didn't give me the sound I was expecting. One of them gave me an excruciating headache every time I tried to play it. So, the weekend was far from a wash (pun intended).

One of the highlights of the weekend was the sweat lodge. This was being led by a South American shaman who was the highlighted guest of the weekend. Some of the participants were pagan and were disappointed that clothing was not optional for this event. Apparently, when pagans experience the sweat lodge and other rituals, they do so in *sky clad* fashion, or clothed only by the sky. I had no intention of embracing this practice, and was more than a bit relieved when the South American shaman insisted on clothing (at least a bathing suit) for the event.

We excitedly gathered at the location while the shamans began to prepare the stone people, the large stones which were being heated in the fire to a certain temperature to create the intense heat needed for the ritual. I imagine it is not unlike saunas, with those stones you pour water on, but in this case, it is done to enhance or create an atmosphere which is supposed to invite altered states of consciousness or religious experiences.

Eventually we were all led into the small structure covered with blankets and other material intended to keep the heat inside the structure. I made sure I was closest to the door, because I was not at all convinced I could stay for the entire ceremony. Leaving in the middle was highly discouraged, but not forbidden.

The facilitators of the event were successful in squeezing twenty people into a structure intended for eleven so needless to say, we were tucked in there like sardines. They told us if we started feeling ill, we could put our heads down to the floor, because that was where it was the coolest.

Unfortunately, the South American shaman in charge began to get exceedingly agitated at the spoiled Americans who wanted out in the middle of ceremony. One participant was obviously under the influence of some drug, and began to argue with the shaman. He was allowed to leave. I will admit I remember very little about the whole event, other than I never wanted to do it again.

The weekend was not a total disaster. My friend and I learned some powerful new shamanic techniques and connected to some very genuine shamanic teachers and mentors through this retreat. But know this: What someone claims to be and what your experience is with those individuals are sometimes different. And just because a hundred or even a thousand people say that a particular ritual is life changing, doesn't mean it will be for you.

Learn from experience.
Trust your instincts.

If you participate in a ritual that you enjoy, do it again! If you don't enjoy it, don't think you need to try it again, assuming maybe next time will be different. There is no rule saying you must enjoy the ritual. I am totally okay with experiencing a sweat lodge one time and one time only. Does that make me less than someone else? No, it just makes me honest.

Do your research.

Do your rituals that are meaningful to you and that give you comfort and hope. Don't judge someone else and the rituals that others choose to incorporate into their spiritual experience. What you experience and what someone else experiences doing the same ritual may be completely different and that does not make either one of you wrong.

Never forget the number one rule of manifesting and rituals: **Do no harm.**

CHAPTER ELEVEN

CROSSING OVER SOULS

Depending on your belief system, you may have opinions concerning what happens when your soul leaves your body. In a previous chapter, I talked of how I tuned in to my Guides and received some information about what really happens when we die. Although the three Guides I talked to each had a bit of a different slant on the subject, none of the communications really contradicted each other. Is it possible that when a body dies, the soul can choose to stay in the earthly realm? Absolutely! There are many possibilities as to why this might happen.

If the death was sudden or traumatic, or if the person was suffering some kind of mental disorder, the soul could be confused. He or she may not be thinking coherently, may not have perceived "the light" as we hear described by many people who have had near death experiences. He or she may not even be aware that they have died, although I have a bit of a hard time understanding how that would happen. But then I am not dead. Or am I?

Here is where it gets a little complicated. When a soul passes, there are a number of things that can happen. The soul can wander around the earthly realm looking for some sense of familiarity. It may be looking for someone it knows. The soul may be trying to right a wrong or trying to find closure on some unfinished business. It may latch on to a living soul who just happens to be around when they pass or someone with whom they have some sort of connection. If the soul had an addiction, it could be looking for someone who is alive and living with a similar addiction, to try to experience their high through them.

Walk-Ins and Attachments

Let's look at a possible scenario. I am not sure how often this happens, but let's say someone dies while in the hospital, and there is someone else in the same hospital who is going in and out of consciousness. The soul of the deceased person could latch on to the living person's body and experience life through that person. This is known as a "walk-in." The original soul of that body may have gone to the other side, or they may still be around in some form. But the soul of the newly deceased latched on to that body and began to live inside it. When the person regains consciousness, he or she may feel different. They may feel a sense of loss or forgetfulness. They also may feel just a bit out of it.

These walk-ins bring validity to the fact that when a body dies, there are sometimes more than one soul attached to it. That sounds really strange, but I once did a reading for a woman who was grieving the loss of her boyfriend. There had been a tragedy of some sort and the boyfriend had killed himself. When I originally tuned in, I did not ask who she wanted to connect with, but I saw two men. I described them to her and she recognized both of them, but pointed out that they had passed years apart from each other. She remembered how when the first one had passed; the personality of her boyfriend had changed. His once outgoing and carefree character had disappeared and he began to act differently. He became a loner, spending many hours inside his rural home, locked away inside himself. He lost weight and began to exhibit behavior that was unlike him before the death of his friend. Eventually, he took his own life.

Despite the fact that the boyfriend and the other person had died years apart, I saw them together. They seemed to be joined to one another.

I surmised that when the boyfriend died, both souls ended up crossing together. However, they had not parted ways even on the other side. I was able to do a separation remotely and free them from one another, allowing them both to go on their way individually.

Be careful what you ask for!!

On another occasion, I tuned in to a woman who had come to me about the son of a friend of hers, who had committed suicide. When her friend called with the news, she immediately ran to her friend's side. She had been there with her through it all, and had even asked God to allow her to carry her friend's pain. Years later she was depressed, and could not forget the event, or the son of her friend. I found the son of her friend in her energy field, and he told me he had attached to her immediately at the scene of the tragedy and had been there ever since. When he passed, instead of going to the light, he had seen the light of her soul and attached to her instead. After that he wanted to go to the light but didn't know how.

There are also stories of how people have gone to the hospital for procedures in which they were put under anesthesia, and when they came out, their personalities had changed. Suddenly they liked different foods, exhibited behaviors that they hadn't previously, and even picked up new habits like smoking or drinking. If a person can find someone to look into their bodies and detect foreign energy, such as myself, then they may recover or go back to the person they were before the event. Often it is as easy as helping the various souls recognize what has happened, and help one or more of the souls to the light, while freeing the original soul to be in the body all by themselves. One of my clients came to me distraught because her husband of many years had gone into a hospital for an operation, and had come out a completely different man. In the end he had an affair, moved the woman into the house with my client, refused to go to counseling or try to work out any details of their inevitable divorce amicably, and ended up losing everything that he and my client had worked years to establish. My job was not to heal this man, but to heal the devastation that his behavior left in its wake.

Unfortunately, sometimes displaced spirits are not limited to adults who happen to find themselves in a vulnerable state. These things sometimes happen when the original souls are children, so when they become adults, they may not even know who they are without the other soul. Many times, imaginary friends are actually souls who attach to children who are open and trusting. Many children are able to physically see souls and may have compassion for them, or even invite them in to cohabitate in their bodies.

Often, the displaced souls just want to tell their stories or finish something that was left undone. By tuning in to them and relating their stories or by having a conversation with them to assist them in finding peace and moving on, they are able to realize they are not helping the soul they have joined. Even if they are not willing to vacate on their own, I am often able to assist the living soul in ridding themselves of these hitchhikers and find peace.

Another possibility, of course, is that everything has its own consciousness. When we receive blood or other body parts from people or even animals, we are inviting into our bodies a form of consciousness that was originally in someone else's body. It is important to be aware of this and act accordingly. You might consider having a conversation with the newly received blood or body part and thanking its original owner for allowing it to be used to enhance your life. I often do this even with the food I eat. Although I recently decided to limit my animal intake, when I do, I am always aware of the energy of the animal from which the food was derived. That chicken or fish was originally its own form of awareness. At some point it was killed to bring me nourishment. I try to remember to thank any consciousness that remains with that animal or at least thank the soul of the animal for sacrificing its life to nourish my own. No, I don't believe we retain the souls of everything we welcome into our bodies, but often there are some remaining bits of consciousness or awareness. It is important to recognize and honor their gift to us. We need to acknowledge that most meat that we buy comes from animals that have been treated poorly. The suffering of the animal may still be attached to the body that it once occupied. If I do decide to consume meat, I apologize for any treatment it received that caused it trauma before I thank it for its gift to me.

Brotherly Love or Fear?

Once I tuned in to a client who was the firstborn after a stillborn child. I found the soul of the dead brother attached to my client's energy field. The client had an unnatural fear of having children, believing that they would be stillborn. I found this to be the fear of the dead brother, not the client. Once I was able to help the stillborn child go the light and find peace, the client was able to release his fear of having children.

Helping souls that are not in their bodies is one of the most rewarding aspects of my healing practice. When I feel a soul go to the light, I experience an inexplicable sense of joy rising up from the deepest parts of my belly. When someone expresses doubt that souls need to be crossed, I have to go back to that feeling of exuberance and joy, knowing that indeed, souls sometimes need help even after their death.

Family Attachments

A recent client of mine had felt the soul of her father who had committed suicide when she was just twelve years old. She related to me that she knew he was on a particular side of her body and she even made sure that when she walked with her husband, he walked on the other side! We were able to release her father's soul to the light and immediately she felt freedom on that side of her body!

A few months later, she came to me for another session. She had suffered many physical challenges in her life, as well as many financial setbacks. She confided in me that she really needed to know the root of these challenges. I immediately connected with her maternal grandmother and great-grandmother. I felt that one or both of them had spent some time in a wheelchair. She confirmed that both of them had, and had suffered many physical challenges for many years.

I also sensed that these ladies were not financially challenged at all. I mentioned to my client that I did not feel her financial challenges were from them and she agreed. I was also given the information that possibly the grandmother was very well off, but had no love in her marriage. Her husband had provided well for her, but was lacking in love. She had made a vow that love was more important than money, and this vow had carried over to the current lifetime for this client. She confirmed that she and her husband loved one another deeply, but always faced financial setbacks. I sensed that her soul and the soul of this ancestor may be the same soul or were extremely connected, and felt the need to have her release the vow that love was better than money. I told her soul that she could enjoy both! We also broke the generational tendency for physical challenges. Some months later I learned that this client had begun a full-time job and had completely shifted her life.

During this same session, I connected with a Native American man who had attached to my client when she was about five. I felt that he was in some way connected to her grandmother's home, where she had spent a lot of time during her childhood. Upon connecting with him, he confessed that he drank a lot and had a gambling problem. He always felt like his life was being drained from him. He suffered from depression as well, which plagued the client on occasion. I felt that possibly the tendency to feel her health and her money being drained away was also connected to this soul. He was not, by the way, related to her at all, as far as I could tell. She did not know of a Native American connected to her grandmother's house, but we were able to send him to the light. She immediately felt lighter when he crossed.

When a soul has been attached to a person from childhood, sometimes the adult person has to re-program their thinking in order to begin their life without the effect of the attachment. In this client's case, I gave her some affirmations to help her.

We can cross over the souls of those who attach themselves to the living, but sometimes the living have to then learn to live their lives without the influence of that soul. If the soul has been with them a long time, it may be difficult for the living to differentiate between their own thoughts and the thoughts of the attachment. When the attachment is gone, the work begins for re-programming the thoughts.

The Light Meditation

Sometimes it is a bit scary to think that we, as living souls, can be influenced in our thoughts by souls that are just hanging around us or attached to our energy field. I have a meditation that I often teach my clients—one that I do myself, and even with my grandchildren—to release any energy to the light that does not belong to us.

If you begin to feel like you are heavy, sad, or angry, when a moment ago you felt fine, you may have been slimed by a passersby's energy. You may have felt the emotions of someone who may or may not be in physical form. We often mistake those emotions for our own and carry them around with us indefinitely. The good news is, if our energy is not compatible with that of sadness or anger, then the energy usually goes away on its own, eventually. However, if we already have a tendency to carry those emotions, then that energy may stick around, due to familiarity.

You can easily send that energy to the light by simply saying,

> **❝ I release any energy that does not belong to me to the light with love. ❞**

Or you can imagine the light that is your soul inside your body shining brightly and filling any empty spaces in your energy field with light, and sending any energy that is not yours to the light.

Children are especially susceptible to "hitchhikers" so you might want to lead your children or grandchildren in this guided meditation frequently. You simply have them imagine the light in their body shining brightly and sending anything that is not characteristic for them to the light with love. It is quick and easy, and many times will help solve behavior issues with children who are unexplainably acting out of character.

Disconnecting Spirits from Children

I had a client whose five-year-old daughter had begun exhibiting interest in sexual experiences. She began talking about situations that were completely inappropriate for a five-year-old to *know* about much less talk about. She was playing with her dolls in an inappropriate way and exhibiting sexual behavior not befitting of a child her age. The mother could not think of any time when the child may have been inappropriately touched or had any actual experiences, although this could not be completely ruled out. I was able to tune into the child's energy field and connect with an entity that was extremely sexual in nature. I was able to disconnect my client's daughter from this entity and send it to the light for healing or re-programming. The inappropriate sexual conduct ceased completely and as far as I know, the child retains no memory of the activity.

It is significant to note that there are many energy forms in the world of Spirit. Some of them have been human and many have not. I was unable to ascertain whether or not this particular entity had ever been human. I do not label any entities as demons due to the preconceived notion we have of what demons are and what they do. But there are many energy forms that seem to have specialties and exhibit specific behaviors. I cannot say specifically if energy forms have specialties but they seem to. Just as a human spirit may have been a piano player but has no knowledge of painting or writing, it seems to be in the spirit world. Many times, if an unsuspecting child happens upon one of these entities, that child may become exceedingly interested in experiences that are out of the norm for them. Children that are sensitive to spirit seem to be more susceptible than others to receiving these entities.

For me, it is fairly easy to cross them over into the light. Energetically, I create a portal of light. I call upon the Benevolent Beings of Lights, others call them Angels, for assistance, or perhaps the loved ones of the lost soul. A hole in the atmosphere is created and they seem to almost always go to the light. After they go, I am not sure what happens but I hear they are escorted to different areas of the light for healing, transformation, and if necessary, re-programming. Sometimes they even come back to say thank you.

If a spirit or energy form seems resistant to going to the light I just request the help of Angels to assist me in the process.

Discontented Spirits

I have noticed themes when non-physical energy forms are around. A lovely bed and breakfast my husband and I recently visited was quaint and filled with every imaginable amenity, but the fellow customers seemed to all be nit-picking and complaining about every little detail. At first, I attributed this malcontent to the social status of the fellow constituents. But as I relaxed in one of the lovely sitting rooms tuning in to the energy in the home, which dated back to the 1830s, I sensed that the discontent could be due to the non-living residents. They seemed to be nit-picking every detail and choice that the owners had made and I sensed that the spirits were as discontented as the customers. The house had been many things—a bank, a restaurant, a tavern, and now an inn—but the spirits seemed discontented about all of those choices. I reasoned with them that perhaps their discontent was because they were not in their rightful places, and maybe they should consider going to the light where they belonged.

The history of the inn tells that this particular home was a haven for Union soldiers during the Civil War. On the other side of the street was the haven for southern sympathizers. The courtyard between was often the middle ground where these two sides fought it out, literally. Obviously, some healing needs to take place for the land and the souls of the deceased who experienced strong, emotionally intense trauma.

On this particular excursion, no souls seemed to present themselves to me to be ready to cross. They insisted on staying and fighting. Perhaps another day.

CHAPTER TWELVE

CHANNELING

Channeling is a word that describes what happens when a living person allows a non-living energy or a spirit of some kind, to use their voice to speak words of which the living person would have no knowledge.

There are many cases of channeling when the human is not in direct knowledge that the non-living is using their body or their voice. I believe many cases of mental illness could possibly be explained by researching a person's sensitivity to the voices of the deceased. Maybe these individuals are continually hearing the deceased or the non-living talking and don't know how to turn it off. I am sure this is not always the case, but many times I believe if we could separate the living from the voices that are talking to them, we could assist them in finding peace.

As a trained sensitive, I will often voluntarily offer up my voice to the non-living for communication. Sometimes this is a deceased person, perhaps a relative of a client, or a friend. Sometimes I offer those souls who are stuck in the in-between place the opportunity to communicate their truth before assisting them to the light. Then again, sometimes the communication is coming from another source, what I like to call my Benevolent Helpers. In this case the communication comes to offer help or healing or even wisdom beyond my own capacity to communicate. Whether I call them Guides, Angels, or Benevolent Helpers, their wisdom is beyond my own and always offers the truth that is needed in a particular situation for healing or assistance.

A Session with Margaret

When I began my session with Margaret, I really did not originally intend to channel the guides directly to her. Her session began as a normal soul healing. She had come to me before so she was familiar with the process. She herself was also a healer and had been instrumental in teaching me many of the healing practices I use.

I began by going into a light trance and connecting with her soul. I normally go to a place in nature and visualize a tree in the middle of a garden. The way the tree appears to me gives me information as to the direction of the session. In this case, the tree was very large and had the face of a Native American man. The top of the tree was black and appeared to be on fire or releasing billowy smoke as you would expect to see from a volcano. The tree was obviously angry.

I sensed the Native American spirit that was a part of Margaret's energy was indignant with the injustices bestowed upon the Native American people. In the branches of the trees were other spirits connected to other causes. I sensed that Margaret had incarnated in many lifetimes, as a soul who had been victimized in some way. In one lifetime she was Native American and her village had been pillaged by white men. In another lifetime, she had fought for the women's movement. In yet another, she had been African American. She had also been a Voodoo priestess at one point. In all of these lifetimes she had intended to bring awareness and justice for the plight of the particular cause to which she connected, and in each lifetime her sense of indignation and anger had smoldered. She had been an activist in each lifetime and despite seeing some results, still felt the injustice and plight of the underdog.

In this lifetime, here and now, her anger and indignation with the injustices in the world completely consumed her. I saw that the tree was deeply rooted and in its branches were nests of various spirits and thought forms, who also felt the emotion of victimization and injustice.

Before I could disconnect her from this huge tree, one of the voices of the divine began to speak and explain to her that anger and retribution could never balance the scales of injustice. Righteous indignation, he explained, could never overcome injustice. The only solution was to realize that the emotions of anger only attracted more of the same. The feeling of victimhood and the self-awareness as a person to whom injustice had been dealt only begat more of the same. There would never be enough money to repay all of the injustices of the world. The only way to overcome it, Spirit explained, would be to stop seeing yourself as a victim. When you see yourself in a certain light, you will attract the experience of exactly what you expect. A prisoner will always be bound by the bars that they create around their own consciousness. As actor *Denzel Washington* once said in one of the most memorable lines what I believe to be in his starring role in *"The Hurricane"* as a wrongfully convicted prisoner, "You can chain up my body but you can never chain up my soul."

This Wise Being of Light began to explain to Margaret that overcoming injustice does not come simply by picketing or marching or bringing awareness to the injustice, although some progress can be made. Just as commiserating with other addicts does not overcome addiction. What you focus on grows. If you spend your days and nights thinking and talking about injustice, that is exactly what you are going to experience. If you spend your time complaining about politicians, government officials, criminals, or anyone else who has profited or benefited at the expense of others, you will find yourself in a constant state of loss. Even the act of being angry about what another healer charges for their services does not result in anything except the loss of abundance in your own experience.

The only thing that overcomes injustice is love and acceptance. Love is the total acceptance of what *is* and the act of finding joy despite any difficulties. Enjoy your life now. Enjoy your experience of happiness and love. Enjoy your loved ones. Enjoy your body. Enjoy the experience of delight in each breath you take and be happy in your body. You may not eliminate world injustice, but you will eliminate it in your own life.

With Margaret's agreement, we were able to release all of the lifetimes of anger and indignation at the injustices suffered both by Margaret personally and by whole sects of society. The Wise Ones were able to show her that feeling injustice, even when suffered by others, and feelings of sympathy for those in pain, does not result in the elimination of that pain. Only love begets love. Joy begets joy. Pain begets pain.

The Wise Ones also acknowledged that many healers and those who call themselves Light Workers had recently become discouraged and were tempted to quit their practices when the world appeared to be going backwards in conscious evolution. Many evil men had come into power and the strides of previous decades of fighting for justice appeared to have come to a screeching halt; even to have begun to go backwards. The Wise Ones told us that the world would always run cycles of good and bad, justice and injustice. The Light would be in power for a while and then it would seem that the darkness would sprout out of nowhere and take over once again.

That is the way of the cycle of light and darkness. The sun shines, then it sets, and the moon begins its trek across the sky. The cycle of light and darkness is intrinsic in our earthly experience and so it would be, for that is the way of the world. The way to find peace within yourself during those times is to simply *be*. Enjoy life for what it is and don't wish to be somewhere else doing something else.

If you simply shine your light, you are doing your part in bringing light to the particular spot in the world where you find yourself. Be happy wherever you are. Shine your light. Decide here and now if you want to be in your body or if you do not. It is not the food you eat or the water you drink which brings life to your body, although it plays a part. Your life exists because you will it to be so. Love each part of your body and choose to be here. You will find contentment and peace.

After the Wise Ones used my voice to transmit this wisdom to Margaret, they assisted in removing the roots of the tree which were imbedded in her energy field. She confessed that she felt the roots of that tree being pulled out all the way to her feet. We sent the energy to the light with love, acknowledging the righteous indignation and the feelings of plight that each individual energy had suffered. Margaret felt great relief as the energy found its way to the light, and we filled the empty spots left behind with love and light.

This was an example of how a healing session can turn into a direct communication from the Higher Intelligence. There are also examples of times when I allowed disembodied souls to use my voice to speak their truth so that they could find peace and go to the light.

The White Table

Early on in my exploration of shamanism, I was exposed to the belief that all spirits need love. This was highly contradictory to my previous experience in Christianity, where we liked to cast out demons, not really even considering where those energies went when we cast them out. In the Bible, Jesus spoke of this, but I never really thought about it until I took a class on de-possession from the shamanic perspective. I learned that all energies need love and yes, you can send a dark spirit to the light, and this is where you *should* send them!

Most of the time we may think an energy is a demon due to the activity that is generated by its presence. But many times, these energies are simply lost or confused souls that just need a voice to speak their truth, and some guidance to help them to the light.

The plain truth is that whatever we focus on grows. We will attract the energies with which we are most energetically compatible. If we are living out our lives with the energy of love and joy, it is highly doubtful we will run into a lot of demons, or mean-spirited ghosts.

Once I learned the art of allowing discarnate souls to speak through my voice, I found that this was a practice I truly enjoyed. I had no fear of those souls taking up residence in my body, because my primary energy frequency is that of love and joy. (A depressed, lonely, or even murderous soul would not have been comfortable for long inside of my body.) They often found peace and closure by expressing their deepest emotions. This allowed them the ability to surrender to the path headed to the light.

One of the first times my husband witnessed me allowing a soul to speak their truth was soon after I had learned a technique practiced in Brazil called the "White Table." We had invited a select group of participants to the gathering. All participants were instructed to wear white clothing and we had placed a white tablecloth on the table where the ritual was to take place. This was so that the souls knew that we were in alignment with the light and were benevolent. I would be allowing spirits to come in who wished to cross over but were being held back by some unfinished business. I would be channeling their conversation to another participant who would be counseling them and encouraging them to cross.

As Clay witnessed me channeling a soul, he became so alarmed and frightened he almost interrupted the session, which would have been a disastrous mistake. In our seventeen years, he has witnessed me cry only a handful of times. I am not a crier. But on this occasion, I found myself sobbing desperately, due to the feelings of loss and despondency felt by the spirit. She had been an early settler who witnessed the death of her family and watched as her house was set on fire by Native Americans. When one of the other participants in this session convinced her that much time had passed and her family was in the light, she willingly surrendered and was led to the light where she was met by her family members. When I set my intention and began to put into motion the ritual, inviting select participants who I felt could assist the souls to the light, I began dreaming of souls lined up at my door and inside my house, waiting for the session to begin.

I have found that spirits are fairly eager to tell their stories. They want to find healing and restoration.

It is my conclusion that there are emotions, souls, and pieces of souls that become stuck in other rooms of reality. They're waiting for someone knowledgeable of their predicament to help them find their way out of that particular room and into a higher state of awareness and peace.

CHAPTER THIRTEEN

PAST LIFE EXPLORATION

B eing brought up Christian, I did not immediately embrace the possibility of such things as past lives. When I let go of my Christian beliefs and began to explore other belief systems, this seemed to present itself over and over for my examination.

In researching the beginnings of Christianity, I discovered that the earliest Christians did in fact believe in reincarnation. After two hundred years or so, it was determined that believing you can try it again if you don't get it right the first time made it more difficult to control people. Fear is what drives a lot of teachings. Fear allows control. If you are afraid of dying and going to hell, you may behave in a manner that is acceptable to those in places of power.

Knowing back then that the earliest Christians believed in reincarnation would have been nice, but when I began my exploration of various beliefs, reincarnation just made sense. Maybe because of me or maybe just coincidentally, my family always seemed to end up in houses that displayed evidence of being haunted. In our Christian days, I would pass it off as a lot of different things but never ghosts.

Napoleon and the Ghosts Downstairs

On one occasion, when my daughter was young, but old enough to be left home alone for short periods of time, I came home from work and she declared to me that whatever was in the basement she had scared it off. She had heard the sliding glass door downstairs open and close, and then heard someone down there moving things around and making a racket. Instead of running to a neighbor or hiding under the bed, she grabbed a butcher knife and went down to investigate. Lo and behold, it was just a spirit, I guess. I was incredulous that she had not had any fear in going downstairs to protect her home at the age of twelve. That is when I decided she was the reincarnation of Napoleon or someone with similar energy. I am not sure why I chose Napoleon at the time, and in retrospect, I am not sure why Napoleon would choose to reincarnate as my daughter, now a single mom with two kids, but subsequent exploration into past lives has brought his name up more than once. Interestingly enough, in my investigation of numerology, I discovered that my daughter and Napoleon have the same exact numbers!

This brings on a whole other topic of the power of words, which I will mention here but not elaborate. As her mother, I declared that she and Napoleon were connected in some way. As the years went on, my daughter encountered other issues, which, in retrospect, may have been avoided if I had not compared her to this important historical figure. Even if we sense certain things about our children or other close relationships, it is important to allow them to have this experience, in this lifetime. We have to be careful when examining previous lives.

But, at the time of my comparing my daughter's energy to that of Napoleon's, I was still very much living my life under the umbrella of thought and belief that we only live one life and after that comes the judgment.

But questions remained.

If our souls are eternal, why would we only have one life to live on the Earth, and then after that, what is there? We get rewarded or punished for eternity based on the choices we made over a seventy- or eighty-year period of time? It just didn't make sense. And then there was my own sense of feeling as though I had done something at some point in time, but knew that I had not done it in this lifetime.

> Have you ever met someone and instantly liked or disliked them?
> Have you ever gone to a place where you have never been but it feels eerily familiar?

When I began to talk to Spirit, I started receiving information that would hint at past lives or even future lives and, sometimes, simultaneous lives.

My childhood fear of water was explained to me by my mother as an incident that happened when I was a baby. She began to let the water out of the bathtub before she got me out of it and I became hysterical. I would have dreams of drowning at different times and different places, and would wake up as if those events had happened to me but I was someone else, in another time and place. Were those past life recollections? Who knows? Nowadays, there are many stories of children having recollections of events from previous lifetimes and some of the information could be verified, including names and locations of which they would have no knowledge in their current incarnation.

Past life exploration is one avenue of my work that people seem to be drawn to. Everyone wants to know who they were in a previous life. But please note, I don't tend to go into past life exploration with the sole intention of entertainment. When I do past life exploration with a client, I like to do it with the intention of solving a puzzle or healing a wound from the current life which cannot be healed any other way. Sometimes I do these explorations for the sole purpose of discovering the origins of a particular issue with which they are dealing, and sometimes it happens during the course of a session that is focused on something else entirely.

The Heart Wants What It Wants

Recently I was in a session with a client and we were healing old wounds and exchanging soul pieces from past relationships. At one point I saw a man sitting on a horse. I knew he was not from this lifetime because of the clothing he was wearing. He seemed to be some sort of royalty, like a knight or a prince perhaps. When I looked through my vision for my client, I found her as a peasant of sorts. She and the man I saw were from different classes of people, and in this period of time I was observing, interacting and certainly falling in love with someone outside of your own class was not allowed.

It almost seemed like a Cinderella story, except it did not have a happy ending. They met, fell in love, and had an intense romantic interlude. Eventually he left her and rejoined his elite life and married someone within his own class. She made a vow, or determined inside herself, that love would always elude her. This event followed her into her current life and soon I had the revelation that this man was the one she was currently dating.

Surprisingly, or not surprisingly, she revealed that whenever she did her personal meditation, she always saw the man she was dating on a horse, although he did not own one or even necessarily like horses. In this lifetime, he was also very well off and she had just recently been laid off from her job. Was this an actual previous life or was it symbolic of this current relationship? There is no way I can say for sure, but I tend to believe we repeat patterns of behavior or events in multiple lifetimes until we resolve the issues that went unresolved. In this lifetime, money and commitment seemed to be obstacles in their relationship. Time will tell whether this relationship finds closure after the healing session.

Just remembering is often not enough. After we discovered this lifetime for my client, we began to rewrite history, at least in her cell memory. I had her re-experience that other lifetime, but in this experience, the man of her dreams ignored protocol and took her home to meet his family. They embraced her with open arms and they all lived happily ever after.

I also talked to the man's cell memories and reminded him that this lifetime was not that lifetime. That lifetime was complete and he was free to live this life and make choices completely different than he had before. Notice I did not cross his free will. I only relieved his cell memory of the prior lifetimes so he could make choices based on the present time.

Crash Landing on Venus

We sometimes only think of past lives lived on this planet, but I once had a spontaneous memory of a lifetime where I crash-landed on Venus. I was deep in meditation when I had the sensation of being on or in a large object that had crashed. Somehow in the meditation I knew it was Venus. When I opened the door and got off the ship there were many other types of beings there from many different places. I tried to see what I looked like, but that was not shown to me. The others all looked very different from each other, and I knew that they were from many dimensions. We were all sitting in a circle and it was time for me to go meet the ruling energy of the planet. When I entered into the room there was nothing but light, and the energy felt magnificently loving. I had never felt such love emanating from anywhere. I wondered if this energy was the energy known as Venus since Venus is the God of Love.

At that point, I spontaneously emerged from my meditation. It was a powerful experience, and one that I had not intended to have. I cannot discount the possibility that although in our dimension Venus is uninhabitable, in other dimensions perhaps that is not the case.

Recalling a Past Life Death

Previously I shared a past life recollection in which I spontaneously found myself atop a structure that Native Americans erected for their dead. This spontaneous memory subsequently worked out in my favor, for I was contacted by a Lakota medicine man in our area asking me what right I had to practice or teach shamanism. He wanted to know what tribe I was from and what my credentials were.

I told him that I had none. I told him about my spontaneous vision that happened during meditation and about knowing that I had practiced shamanism in a previous lifetime. His attitude immediately changed and he gave me the Lakota name *Ska Kanga*, which means White Crow. As it turns out, the vision meant something to him and he said that healers often have the power animal of a white crow. He has been nothing but supportive since.

What are some clues to past lives you may have lived?

If you have any extreme likes and dislikes, with nothing in this lifetime that leads to a point of entry, the indication is strong that you may have had a past life where you first developed that strong opinion. If you have an unnatural fear of something, like water in my case, chances are good your cells may be remembering a prior lifetime. You may meet someone and instantly like or dislike them. You may be intensely attracted to an area of the world or a time period.

When I was young, I was extremely good at drawing. I remember being in kindergarten and everyone in the class, including the teachers, enjoyed watching me as I drew pictures. Finger painting made no sense to me. My drawings were real and detailed. I imagine I had developed that skill in a prior lifetime.

If you are born knowing how to do something, or knowing things that are not in the typical knowledgebase for someone your age, you are probably remembering a prior lifetime in which you developed that skill or ability. It is highly likely that we have all lived many, many lifetimes. It is also likely that not all of them have been on earth.

I have had more than one out-of-body experience in which I found myself in other dimensions or possibly other planets. Many of my Guides do not look like they are human but look instead like pillars of light. I imagine that they are from wherever I have been in my meditations. They are always benevolent and offer only information and guidance that is loving and empowering. It's also possible that I am connecting with my Higher Intelligence.

It is also possible to see future lifetimes.

Time only exists in our dimension. I believe that when we decide to reincarnate, we choose what time period in which we want to live. This is difficult for our linear minds to understand, but it only stands to reason that if time and space don't really exist, then the possibility of living the past, present, and future simultaneously, is real. Just by shifting our awareness a little bit and then trusting the information, it is within the realm of possibility that we can experience a future lifetime or even a simultaneous lifetime in some other realm of existence.

Simultaneous Lifetimes?

On at least one occasion and possibly two, I have met someone who I had a sneaking suspicion was actually me, living my life in just a little bit different version of myself. Does that sound too spooky for you? Obviously, I did not tell them but the fact is, we are all connected. We are all sparks of the Divine, choosing to live out our awareness in different versions of consciousness. Technically I am you and you are me in the largest sense of this perspective. If we are all just drops of water in the same ocean, then the awareness that is one drop of water, should easily be able to connect to the awareness in another drop of water. Just by connecting to one another, we can share our wisdom and our insights in a loving and empowering way. How much better to empower one another with our visions of empowerment and awareness, rather than tearing one another down and judging one another! Let us all hold visions of each other being our best selves, and overcoming all obstacles that present themselves!

Past-life recollection does not have to be administered by a licensed past-life therapist, although I am not saying you should not go that route. You can do guided meditations to take you to your own past lives, or you can just ask your Higher Guidance System to help you. You may have dreams or spontaneous memories that just present themselves to you. Trust the information. Write it down. Meditate on it. See if it rings true for you.

Whether the memories that present themselves to you are real or imagined doesn't really matter as long as you receive important information that better equips you to live your life in present time. If you receive an answer to a nagging question, a spontaneous healing, or just generally feel better, what does it matter if the memory was real or imagined? If it was imagined, then your Higher Guidance System was just using an analogy to give you insight into your life and your current state of affairs. Isn't that what Jesus did when he told parables?

CHAPTER FOURTEEN

TAROT AND OTHER DIVINATION TOOLS

Nowadays, the tarot cards are one of my favorite divination tools, but in the beginning, I was not interested in learning them. I was pretty confident in my ability to give Spirit messages without any props or tools and to me, learning the meaning of seventy-eight cards and all of the possible combinations did not interest me.

But Spirit had other ideas.

Whenever Spirit wants to give me a message with which I am not completely on board, I find that the message comes through more than once. Sometimes I have to receive a message multiple times, especially if I am skeptical of any particular message. This time was no exception. The first episode was during a meditation. I was doing my daily meditation when I heard the word "Isis." This was before the infamous terrorist group stole her name, but I knew this name to be that of an Egyptian Goddess. At least I knew I had heard or read the name somewhere. I did not really know who she was or what her specialty was, and I certainly did not know if she knew anything about tarot cards. I connected with her energy and asked what her message to me was.

In a very straightforward manner, she proclaimed that she had come to teach me to read tarot cards. I politely thanked her, but told her I really was not interested. I came out of my meditation and promptly looked her up on Google. I never found any indication that she was associated with the cards, although there is a thread of thought that the ancient cards may have originated in Egypt. Even this claim is widely disputed. Over the course of the next few weeks, Spirit bombarded me with messages about learning the cards. Eventually I conceded.

While I was learning the cards, I had a blog in which I wrote messages from Spirit. I used this as a platform for receiving messages via the cards. I would draw a card, listen to Spirit for a message, and publish the message and a picture of the card. I really didn't take any classes or study a great deal other than listening to my own intuition and writing down what I heard.

Now I publish on social media a Card of the Day based on tarot cards or other divination tools and often use the cards when doing readings. It seems like some people need the visual of a picture describing the message that comes to me. Many times, I will give a direct message first and then use the cards as a backup. Most of the time, the cards will complement my readings or further explain what Spirit has already told me.

Dreaming the Cards

Spirit also occasionally gives me a dream that, upon awakening, I realize is a depiction of one of the cards. The first time this occurred, I dreamed of the tower which is one of the most ominous of the cards. The picture shows a man and a woman falling head first out of a tower that has been struck by lightning and the roof appears to be on fire. Traditionally, this card represents having an experience or event that completely upsets your world. Sometimes it represents learning a truth that creates chaos. At times it is necessary to tear things down that have already been built, in order to start anew.

In my dream, my husband Clay and I were on the upper floor of a building. When we became aware that the roof was on fire, Clay threw me out the window and then jumped out himself. When I was safely out of the building, I realized that I had left my purse inside. Setting aside logic, as we often do in dreams, I ran inside, grabbed my purse, and escaped to safety without harm. Later in my waking state, I knew that we were about to experience a challenge, but because I was able to retrieve my purse, which represents my identity, finances, and everything of importance, I knew that I would be okay.

Within a day or two of the dream, we learned a difficult truth about a close family member. The experience definitely upset our world and caused us a tremendous amount of grief, but we have weathered the storm with minimal effects to our bottom line.

About a year before I made the decision to retire from the Post Office, I had a dream involving the two of swords. This card is all about not having enough information to make an informed choice between two options or putting off a decision until later. I had been contemplating retiring from my day job and the decision had me in a bit of a pickle. My soul was ready to embark upon the next adventure and make my living doing readings, classes, and events, but the logical side of me still kind of liked the regular paycheck I received twice a month. The thought of being completely surrendered to Spirit for my livelihood scared the bejesus out of me!

I woke up knowing exactly why I had dreamed of the card. The card talks about putting off a decision until a later date or until further information is available. A day or two after I dreamed of the card, I learned of a supplemental income for which I would be eligible if I waited an extra year to retire. I felt relieved and decided to put off retirement for another year.

A lot of people fear the cards due to society, religious scare tactics, or just fear of the unknown. The cards really have no inherent evil or energy of their own. They simply contain pictures that tell stories about life. Yes, some of the cards look scary, but sometimes life is scary. If you take out all of the cards that could be interpreted as ominous, you remove a good portion of life experiences. The truth is, sometimes difficult messages need to be told.

Sometimes I will see a particular card when I am doing a reading, or I will be talking to a Spirit and realize it is the spirit of a particular card. Just this morning during my meditation I began to hear a voice speaking in a

British accent. When I asked who was speaking to me, I had a visual of a king. I spoke to him for a few minutes and then saw one of the king cards of the tarot. I realized that I was being given an additional insight into the attitude and thought processes of kings. (I did study British history a bit in school but that has been forty years ago! I was not completely sure which British king was speaking to me but I imagine if it was important, he would have told me.) This will add to my understanding of the king cards when I draw them. I also have some relatives whose last name happens to be King so there are a lot of possibilities for shades of meaning to those particular cards.

It is nice to have helpers on the other side who know which chapter of my life I am going to be working on. Thankfully they just show up and give me stories and insight into particular aspects of what I am going to be thinking about, experiencing, or working on during any particular moment of time.

The cards of the tarot are also good tools to use when a question is posed to me to which I am given no direct answer. I have never found the cards to be wrong. Sometimes the timing is off, sometimes I may interpret them wrong, but the cards are almost always correct.

Almost always, you say? Well, here is how the cards work. The cards sense your energy, your thoughts, and your focus. If you are saying one thing and thinking something else, you may get a mixed reading. Or, if I am attempting to post my card of the day and my hubby is watching the news or something else is going on in the background, the cards may come up having to do with the news or what is going on around me rather than the message I am trying to receive. Sometimes the cards will simply be playing with me or describing something that is happening at the time.

A Picture is Worth a Thousand Words

Once, during the time period when my husband owned a health food store, I was in the store decorating for an upcoming holiday. I was standing on a chair when I noticed an old friend and his acquaintance. The two of them approached and we talked for a bit. After they left, I got down off the chair and went into the room where all the decorations were staged, and also where I had my purse. Apparently in the shuffle, my purse had fallen over and my cards had fallen on the floor. All of them were face down, save one card, the three of pentacles. The picture on the card shows a man standing on a bench and two people standing close by looking up at him. The card symbolizes cooperation, working together on a project, or being admired for your skills in a certain area. In my case, the card identically matched my experience from a few moments before, when two people stood and talked to me as I stood on a chair. The card did not have a message specifically, except maybe, "Ha-ha, we see what you are doing and we have a card for that"!

The Tower Redefined

On another occasion, I was reading the cards for a client. The cards were talking about the purchase of a house. This seemed to be a good decision for the client, but the cards were indicating being wary of some particular institution, of which I initially was stumped. The tower card had come up. We had already ascertained that the purchase of the home was a good decision. What did it mean? With a little questioning, I learned that the name of the bank with whom she was planning to get a mortgage was Tower Bank. I suggested she may want to do some research before committing herself to that bank.

I guess you can say that sometimes my use of the cards is traditional and sometimes not so much, but really, there are no rules as to the use of the cards. I believe they take on the energy of the person who holds them. Spirit is continually giving me new ways to use the cards to give and receive messages with them.

Raped by a Ghost?

I recently had a client email me and suggest that she may have been raped by a ghost. She woke up in her bed with her inner thighs sore and moist, the aroma of vaginal fluids, and a sense of intrusion. Because of my schedule, it would be a couple weeks before I could make it to her house, but offered to tune in remotely and then come in person at a later time. She had inquired of her boyfriend, asked if he had visited her room, and received a negative response. When remotely tuning in to her bedroom, I didn't sense any spirits, but had a sense of impropriety. Trying to get further details, I turned to the cards. I chose an ace of cups, which normally represents the beginning of a new relationship. I looked at the card and was immediately drawn to the picture of the cup with a dove depositing a wafer into the cup. My first reaction was to wonder if the boyfriend had possibly dropped something in her drink.

I emailed the client back and suggested that possibly something not so paranormal may have happened, and that she needed to first explore the possibility that the intruder was not a ghost. I inquired if her boyfriend has given her a drink before bedtime. With no explanation, she cancelled our proposed meeting date. I have no way of knowing if she was offended at my suggestion, or if she had discovered a difficult truth.

Sometimes I will see in my mind's eye a particular card when I am giving a message or when I am doing a soul healing. The card will tell me what area to focus on in the client's reading or healing, or maybe just give me some insight into a particular area of their life.

My Guides have also given me direction in using the cards to read chakras, to use the bagua map (a feng shui tool) to receive guidance into various areas of a client's life, and other interesting but not-so-traditional uses for the cards.

Using the cards to talk to the dead

Recently I used the cards as a means of connecting with a client's mother who had recently passed. I had my client pick a card and let her mother know that the card would be significant in some way or provide a message for her daughter. This tool is valuable if I initially have trouble connecting with a client's loved one (which happens sometimes) or just for fun.

The client picked the nine of cups, which depicts a man sitting in front of a table in which there are nine cups. The man has his arms crossed and the idea is that he is pretty pleased with himself.

The client's mother said that she was pleased with how her life had turned out, and felt proud of her daughter and other members of the family. She had been surprised and pleased at how many people turned out for her memorial service. She said that the loving conversations she witnessed and the expressions of love and appreciation for her were overwhelming and significant. She had not realized she had touched so many lives. It made her feel closure and assisted her in moving on.

The client agreed that her memorial service had been a wonderful experience. Many people showed up to express their condolences and the family had been surprised at the turnout. The client left feeling satisfied that her mother had indeed been present and given the message to her. She felt comfort knowing that her mother had received such a sendoff and that it had assisted her in moving on.

It seems as time goes on, I develop a particular relationship with the images on the cards. They take on a personality of their own and they will give me meanings that one would never find in a traditional book of card interpretations. I have a card that represents our current president and there are times when this card comes up while I'm giving a reading. This tells me that the client may have an interest in politics. I also have a card that represents my relationship to my cat. The possibilities are endless.

Rock Divination

Using tools to divine answers is as old as caveman drawings, and the earliest of conceptions of the need to receive guidance beyond our own five senses. One of the first tools I learned to use was rocks.

I was taught in my studies of shamanism that everything has its own consciousness and its own soul. This is why when we use natural objects like stones and crystals in our spiritual practice (I would like to suggest that tools of Spirit need not be objects you buy in a store), there are times when they seem to disappear and then reappear at some point in the future in a different location. I can't tell you how many times I have given crystals to clients who subsequently lost them. I have a problem keeping a pendulum. The pendulum will work with me for a while and then it will disappear.

My husband once found one of my lost pendulums wrapped around the stabilizing pieces of wood on our kitchen chairs. That particular pendulum had been missing for over two years.

When using a rock or other natural object to divine an answer, think of the question you have in mind while holding the rock that has agreed to be used for this purpose. After the question has been asked, begin to look at the rock for images that seem to appear in the crevices or formations of the rock. As you think about your question and the picture that shows up for you, you will usually be able to interpret the answer to your question.

Pendulums are a bit different. The swing of the pendulum will indicate a yes or a no, and with skill, you can even divine more complicated answers depending on how you word the question.

Once again, the natural objects will let you know if they want to be used for divination or healing. If not, respect their choice.

In one specific session with a client, I used a pendulum to discern the health of her chakras. On the days she was supposed to come for a session, every pendulum disappeared. The only thing I could find that remotely resembled a pendulum was one of those decorative objects that you hang from ceiling fans. When I inquired if I could use it as a pendulum, it politely declined. The session ended up going in a different direction and the use of a pendulum was not required after all.

Asking permission

When choosing a natural object to use in spiritual practice, I always ask permission first. I ask the object if I can use it for a specific purpose, then wait for a *yes* or *no* answer to pop in my head. Sometimes I get a little tingle in the palms of my hands which is a system Spirit and I have for yes/no answers. If I feel a tingle in my left hand, the answer is *no*. If I feel it in my right palm, the answer is *yes*.

In the beginning, I would pick up a rock and look it over, hold it in my hand, perhaps examine the markings on the rock, in order to determine if it felt happy to me. Sometimes I would look at the rock for the possibility of seeing a smiley face. I could see a smile or a frown almost every time. If I saw a smile, I would take it home. If I saw a frown, I would put it back.

This is also how a person might use tea leaves or even clouds as divination. I would ask the question either out loud or in my head. Then I would examine the object or the cup of tea leaves for formations that appear to me to resemble something in particular.

Cloud Divination

Once I was tuning in for a client while I was driving (I don't recommend this but all of us sensitives probably do it) and noticed a formation in the clouds that resembled a baby carriage. I immediately knew that the client's grandmother had been extremely controlling during an incident involving her when she was a baby. Obviously, she did not remember the event, but she was able to ask some family members and confirm a volatile situation involving her as an infant, and her grandmother.

There was a period of time when death seemed to be more common than not in the family. I was having frequent dreams involving babies in water. My interpretation of that dream is that someone is going to die. Every time I dream it, someone I know dies, or a family member of someone I know dies. (Hey, everyone has their symbols, and this is mine.) One day I was driving and looked up in the clouds and saw a baby who appeared to be swimming. My daughter called not too long after that, and let me know that the father of my grandson had passed.

Currently my two favorite tools are a magnet and a pendulum. With the magnet I am able to "pull" energy, emotions, beliefs, and fears right out of a person's energy field. Although at first, I was skeptical, the use of the magnet has been invaluable, accurate, and effective. With the pendulum I can shift energy, determine how compatible I am with a client, remove entities, clear homes, and perform an endless array of energy clearing tasks. Sometimes I just don't have my sage with me or burning it is in some way inappropriate. A pendulum can travel with me wherever I go and it usually does!

Recently I was at an event where a pregnant friend reported debilitating migraines. I pulled out my pendulum and did a little work on her energy field. When I checked back in with her a couple of weeks later, she was happy to report that she had not had a migraine since that time!

Why does it work?

I asked my Guides why the pendulum seemed to be such a powerful healing tool. Although many people use it only for divination, I have found that divination is only a fraction of its beneficial uses.

The Guides indicated to me that a great deal of energy work is done in the astral planes, or the fields of energy that are in a close but alternate frequency field. When we use the pendulum, we are pulling the energy of the work we are doing in that field into the earth realm. The pendulum itself comes from the earth, often a crystal or heavy object of some kind, and the air creates the movement. A pendulum uses two elements of the earth plane, air and earth to pull energy into this dimension from the higher frequencies. That is why it is important when doing healing work to bring the healing into the physical body experience through some kind of ritual or physical movement. If you don't use a pendulum, do a ritual of some kind or use movement to bring the healing into the physical body experience.

Whether we use tarot cards, rocks, pendulums, or other tools to enhance our spiritual practice or not, it is important to remember that these tools are reacting to the energy field of the person who is using them. It is important to be aware that any information or healing that comes from using the tools are limited in scope to the energy or frequency of the human channel. We are the conduits of the energy but the connection to the Higher Frequencies is limited in scope to our own personal accumulated energy. It is important for us to constantly be purifying our energy fields so that we can be pure channels for the energy so that what we provide is both accurate and beneficial. The spirits around us are also in various stages of purification and frequency so we can only attract nonphysical energies that are a match to our individual frequency. Do you ever wonder who it is that is giving you the information? Do you worry that you are channeling energies that are not beneficial?

If you are constantly in a lower vibrational frequency, feeding your body unhealthy food or substances, not exercising, engaging in arguing or gossip, aligning yourself with unhealthy organizations that are transmitting the energy of division, hatred, or tribalism, or even filling your mind with too much negative television or music choices, you will be bringing forth the energy of that with which you are most aligned.

CHAPTER FIFTEEN

DREAMS

Dreams are one of the ways Spirit chooses to communicate with us. Most of the time our dreams are symbolic and represent life experiences or emotional struggles we may be having. Our dreams also tend to use symbolism that we have created in our waking life. In my previous chapter on the tarot I talked about two dreams I had that depicted cards of the tarot.

It is perfectly understandable that I would have dreams of tarot cards. I would be surprised if someone who was not educated in the cards of the tarot began to dream of the cards. Spirit sends us messages through dreams, songs, symbols, or visuals based on information in our own experience. Sometimes dreams are simply our brains rebooting all the information that has been presented to it during the course of a day. If we think of our minds as computers, and every thought, visual, sound, taste, smell, or touch as input that is being entered into that computer, you can imagine there would be an overload of information, if not for our sleep time.

Sleep has long been thought of as the time when the soul can free itself of the constraints of a human body. During sleep, our souls can fly into distant lands, even distant universes. A cord of energy holds our souls to our bodies so that we remember to come back.

Have you ever woken from a deep sleep and needed a minute to figure out where you were and what was happening? That is because when you awake from a sleep state your soul is immediately called back into your body. If your soul was on Venus, for example, it would have a long distance to travel to get back in your body in a matter of seconds. However, this isn't too difficult since your soul, unencumbered by a human body, can travel at the speed of thought.

Our dream state is also the time when we are most susceptible to and accepting of messages and contact from the spirit world. Have you ever had a dream about a loved one who is on the other side? I get that question all the time and the answer is yes. That dream is your loved one sending you a message.

Message from Mom

Right before my mother passed away, she asked that when she passed, I would place my dad in an assisted living facility at the Veterans Hospital in Florida. She was convinced he would be unable to care for himself and did not want to place the burden of his care on my sister and myself. Dad was obviously not on board with this directive, so my sister and I let him decide for himself. He chose to continue living in the adult community where he and my mom had spent so many years together. My mom sent me a dream asking me why we had not followed her instructions. Yes, she was still trying to handle earthly affairs from the other side.

On another occasion I had a dream of my mother at a party. The room was filled with cigarette smoke and there was a huge crowd of people dancing, drinking, and making merry. In life, my mother never would have been in this environment. Being devout born-again Christians, we were not allowed to go to fairs, carnivals, movies, and certainly not a party like this

When I saw my mother in the dream, she was smoking a cigarette and she may have even had a drink in her hand! What?! I remember walking up to my mom in the dream and demanding to know why she was here in this environment. Her answer to my question obviously reflected her disappointment in her faith's lack of ability to heal her of the cancer that killed her. "When I was alive," she explained, "I did everything right. And look, I died anyway."

After Mom passed, my dad became very independent, and I believe the last years of his life ended up being his most vibrant. He began to walk, socialize, do his own laundry, and balance his own checkbook. Even his lifelong health issues seemed to improve.

I almost knew when he was going to pass. I didn't know the exact date, but I knew that I was going to be taking a trip and that Dad was slowing down in his ability to function.

When he fell at my sister's house and hit his head, she called with the news. She didn't know how bad it was, but thought maybe I should come down. On the way, I was listening to the radio and a song came on talking about seeing the light. I had a vision of Dad going into the light. I had to pull over and allow the emotions to run their course before continuing on the long journey from my home in Virginia to Florida where he lived. After a difficult couple of weeks, he passed.

While he was in the hospital from the fall, he was in and out of consciousness, and blood was collecting in his brain. My sister and I had to decide whether or not to discontinue his feeding tube and disconnect his pacemaker. I was riddled with guilt. I felt like I was deciding to kill my father. My sister, ever the wise one, must have heard my thoughts. I had not expressed them to her, but at the moment I thought, *I am killing my father,* she said, "Joy, it's not like we are killing him." She also saw white light over his bed.

Dad's Moving On

After he passed, I dreamed I was driving a car and he was in the passenger seat. We stopped at a convenience store and he opened the door and got out. In the dream he was excited to be going in to shop. He couldn't wait to get out of the car. He quickly said goodbye and walked in the store.

This dream was telling me he was excited for his next adventure. I was happy that he was happy, and although some days I still feel the guilt of the decision to unhook his life support, I know he is happy on the other side. He comes through frequently and likes to participate in my healing sessions.

Night at the Oscars

Recently I dreamed that I was attending a night at the Oscars. Anyone who was anyone was there. There were some actors who had already received their Oscars and some were still waiting, as the ceremony was still in progress. In the dream, some sort of cataclysmic event occurred to cause everyone to leave quickly, leaving their Oscars behind.

The interesting part of the dream was that although I knew I was at the Oscars, the award statues looked different from the traditional gold ones. Each one was an exact representation of the person who had received it. I was only an observer and I remember looking at the statues and marveling at how the winners, in their haste to leave the building, had left behind these accolades to their achievements. When I awoke, the dream was so vivid that I began to wonder if I was actually just remembering something I had seen on television.

Symbolically, we could say that the Oscars represent our desires for honor or recognition from our peers, for our achievements. It is that need to have validation and recognition by others, for what we are doing with ourselves and even for our own identities as people. The fact that people were leaving without their awards could possibly mean that mankind is recognizing and awakening to the fact that outer achievement is shallow and not a long-term satisfaction of who we are as individuals. It may not even reflect the truth of our being. The dream could also represent that when we leave this life, we leave behind the recognition and remembrance for everything we have achieved in life behind us.

Although many dreams are messages about our own lives, I was just an observer in this dream, so I don't think it was a reflection of my own thoughts and feelings, but an observation of mankind in the middle of the awakening process. At the time I wondered if there would be a significant event at the actual Oscar awards ceremony, but that did not turn out to be the case.

I have spoken with people who said they received important messages through their dreams and there are even books written on the subject. One woman was given the news through a dream that she had breast cancer. Even the location and size of the tumor was related through the dream. Despite trips to several doctors, no one believed her, and all the tests to prove the validity of the dream came back normal. Finally, she was able to find a doctor who administered a test that targeted the exact spot where she claimed the cancer resided, and this time her suspicions were confirmed.

In the years when I was struggling to maintain my sanity in the midst of a tumultuous life experience, I often had dreams of being in some sort of vehicle with no steering and no brakes. The dream was my confirmation that I felt out of control and helpless to make changes that would make things better.

Later, after I finally took matters into my own hands and changed my living situation, I began having dreams of being lost or being in a maze, unable to find my way out. At that time in my life I had set aside my gift and was trying to live normally. My soul was feeling lost, I suppose, as I tried to reinvent myself and discover how to once again feel like my life had meaning and purpose. Once I acknowledged my gift, I had to figure out how to be a mouthpiece for Spirit, so the dreams continued for quite some time.

When the dreams of being lost subsided, I began to have dreams of being on a highway in some sort of vehicle that was extremely slow or nonfunctioning. I found myself on a bicycle that had a flat tire or in a toy car. This symbolized my impatience with reaching my intended goal to be a Spirit communicator.

Now that I have been successfully delivering messages from Spirit for several years, these recurrent dreams seem to have subsided. I find myself juggling multiple tasks in my dreams, or traveling with too much luggage that I can't seem to handle by myself. This represents the need to delegate or release control, and maybe to clean up some clutter.

As you can see, dreams can be messages from our souls, our loved ones, our Guides, and even Ascended Masters. Years before I decided to leave my Pentecostal belief system and branch out on my own, I had my one and only dream of Jesus.

Jesus in my Dreams

I was standing in line to be baptized at a river. The line was extremely long and I was anticipating a long wait. Then I saw Jesus! He walked up to me and began to speak. Obviously, no one else in the dream saw him or there would have been a crowd drawn to him. I was the only one he approached, but then again, it was my dream.

"What are you doing?" He asked.

"I'm standing in line to be baptized," I replied.

"Well, you can stay here if you want to, but I am going to Greece." Then he began to walk away. I followed him and soon after, the short dream was over. But what a message!

At the time, I thought maybe I was supposed to take a trip to Greece, but at that time in my life, there was no way to get the money to go. Every day was a struggle just to have a roof over our heads and food in our bellies. So, I began to contemplate the symbolism of Greece in the Bible.

When Paul went to Greece, he was unable to convert many there to Christianity due to their fascination with various belief systems and their ideas of many gods. Jesus was just another belief system to explore. I believe the dream was a foretelling of the upcoming dark night of the soul, when I would leave Christianity and begin to explore other belief systems. Jesus was telling me it was all right.

A lot of times dreams contain symbols that are clues to the important messages from Spirit. They almost resemble a game from Spirit. When you wake from a dream, write down everything you can remember from the dream. Even if dreams seem nonsensical, the different aspects of the dream contain clues that give you wisdom and advice from your soul, your Guides, and even your chosen deities.

I won't spend the time here to go over all the symbolism in dreams, for there have been entire books written about that. The important thing to remember is that they are *your* dreams. You may have symbols that mean something entirely different than what you might read in a book or research on the internet. Just like I had to really think about and understand what Jesus was telling me about Greece, dreams may take some awake-time contemplation. Sometimes you won't know for many years what your dreams might be telling you. That is why it is extremely important to write it down.

Dream of a Haunted House

Many years ago, I had a dream involving a house. In the dream, my husband and I and his paranormal team were in the backyard sitting around just chatting. At some point my husband and one of the other team members walked out into the woods that surrounded our yard. They happened upon a house that I did not recognize, and the location of the house was unfamiliar to me as well. Nothing out of the ordinary, you say? Not really, except that the dream was very vivid and although I experienced it many years ago, I remember from the dream what the back of this house looked like. Which brings me to the next story.

Not too long ago my stepson built a house on a wooded lot just outside the city limits. We had been to his property in the beginning stages and all through the process of the building. One day my husband and I were visiting the property and walked around to the back of the house. As I was standing there, I suddenly realized that this was the house in the dream I had had so many years before. But why was the paranormal team there in my dream?

Apparently, my stepson and others have experienced a couple of paranormal incidents. On one occasion when Clay and I were there, we heard a woman's voice. I was the only woman present and I had not said a word. Other of my stepson's acquaintances have also reported some out-of-the-ordinary experiences at that location. At this point we have no explanation for the importance of this dream or this house. Time will tell.

Over time, I have learned a few things about my own dreams that give clues to what they mean. Houses represent our souls. The floor that the dream happens on is significant. The basement represents our subconscious. The main floor is our life in the earthly realm. Different rooms can represent different things. The upper floor or the attic often, but not always, represents our connection to the Divine.

As I previously mentioned in the chapter on tarot cards, I once had a dream where the top floor was on fire. That is because in the tarot, there is one card that contains a picture of a tower and the top portion is on fire. The dream was indicating to me that a difficult truth was about to upset our world. Water represents our emotions and also spirit. Sometimes it can represent money.

Dreams of Poop!

One of the funny analogies in dreams is the dream of poop. I often used to have dreams of poop. The scenarios in the dreams were different but there was poop somewhere in the dream. I really didn't understand the meaning until one day my mentor called. She had had a dream of me and poop. She said it was a sure sign that money was coming my way. Who knew?!

Animals in dreams can mean different things, but if you think about the identifying characteristics of the animal that may give you a clue to their message to you.

I mentioned before that when I have a dream of a baby in water, someone dies. It may be someone close to me or someone I know or know of, so that leaves the door wide open. Usually it is someone fairly close to me or close to a loved one.

One thing that helps you receive messages from your dreams is to ask a question right before bed. Write down what you remember of your dreams the minute you wake up. It may take some time to get the answer but after a while you will get better at it.

It also helps to write down as many dreams as you can, and to create your own personal symbol dictionary. That way Spirit knows which symbols mean what to you, and they will use them repetitively. Now that

I know my symbol of a baby in water is death, each time I dream of that, it will always mean the same thing.

I recently had a dream in which a horse was running around in our house. In the dream I remember wondering where he came from and how did I not know we had a horse? I wondered who had been feeding him. Spirit has a sense of humor. They know that I am always trying to figure out details and sometimes miss the symbolism.

It took some contemplation on my part when I awoke, but I soon realized the horse represented the soul of my husband. When he was doing a lot of spirit investigations, he used to find that, upon listening to the recorders he had running during the long nights spent sitting in the dark, he often heard a horse neighing in unlikely places. I knew intuitively that his spirit totem was a horse. He was at first resistant to this suggestion, as he is not drawn to horses in any way and is sometimes even averse to the thought of humans riding horses for pleasure. He says we are forcing our will upon unwilling participants in the interaction. Unfortunately for my husband, we don't pick our spirit animals. They pick us. And the horse had chosen him.

If someone else dreams of a horse, it is likely to have a completely different interpretation, but I knew the horse represented my husband's soul and his longing for freedom but feeling constrained, as a horse might feel if confined in a small house.

Dreams of Past Lovers or Friends

If you find yourself dreaming of a past friend or lover, it may be a sign that your souls are still connected in some way, or that the person you are dreaming about is talking to you or thinking about you.

Sometimes I have found it necessary to speak to the souls of people who continually show up in my dreams and break the *soul ties*, or cords of energy that link my soul to theirs in an unhealthy way. Most people don't know that they can do this. Remember that you are the director of your own life story and if you don't like the characters or the episodes that continue to show up in your story, you can change it.

I was once told by Spirit that one of the best ways to communicate with the souls of the living is to speak to their souls when their bodies are sleeping. It is fairly easy. Just go into a light trance or meditation state and imagine that they are standing in front of you. State your case clearly and decisively. If you need to apologize, make amends, or create boundaries, this may be the way to go if you are not in a position to speak to their waking consciousness. I found by experience that my soul conversations with the sleeping resulted in changes in the waking relationships I had with those people. Difficult relationships seemed to disappear and relationships that needed closure seemed to resolve themselves.

I still sometimes dream of friends from long ago with whom I enjoyed soul connections. We connect, talk, catch up perhaps, and then we both wake up and go on with our lives. Our souls are not bound by time and space as our bodies are. Our souls are also more willing to put aside grievances. Sometimes grievances are resolved while in the dream state.

Did I save a woman's life in my dreams?

At least one time in my life I dreamed of an event and then saw it on the news the next morning. In this dream I was on the side of a busy road having a conversation with another woman. It seemed the conversation was intense, and at one point we were interrupted by a collision happening on the road behind us. Suddenly I had to pull the woman out of the way of a large truck which struck a car. The intensity of the event woke me up and I remember being annoyed that I was unable to finish the conversation with the woman.

The next morning, I was watching the news while getting ready for work and saw on the television a report of a collision between a truck and a car. The truck dragged the car down the road for several hundred feet before coming to a stop. The news crew was commenting on the extraordinary survival of the woman in the car. Immediately I realized that in the dream, I had pulled the woman out of harm's way. The conversation I was having with her was not the important part. It was the part where I pulled her away from the collision. Am I saying that I saved a woman's life while in the dream state? I don't know, but it certainly appears that way. Our souls are free when our bodies are sleeping. That is all I am saying.

I also once dreamed of being in a getaway car while thieves were in a store robbing it. Was I really there or did I just watch something similar on the television the night before? I can say with confidence that I considered the television possibility and could find no correlation. You could say that the dream state is just another room from the waking state. Who is to say which one is real and which one is an illusion?

CHAPTER SIXTEEN

OMENS

An omen is a warning of a difficult situation coming into our experience. It may be a suggestion to take a different route than usual on the drive home. It could be a dream, a feeling in the pit of your stomach, a sign of some sort, a panic attack, or a combination of all of these. Sometimes Spirit will send us signs many months ahead of a difficult experience to warn or prepare us for what is to occur.

It's Not Your Time to Die

My husband had a near death experience which was shown to me through various signs many months before it occurred. I began to have panic attacks and receive a multitude of signs which, together, warned me of this difficult experience that was coming up. After several months of receiving signs and warnings, I took action. While Clay slept, I spoke to his soul and told him it was not his time to die.

Why does Spirit sometimes give us months of signs before the actual event? I always say, for me, at least, maybe I am a slow learner. One sign, I may think is a coincidence or just a fluke. But a combination of signs,

I am more likely to take notice. I also have this thing about free will. At the time of my husband's event, I didn't care about free will. I will admit I did not give his soul a choice. I told him it was not his time to die.

About a year later, Spirit told me that at some point I needed to give my husband's soul the choice to decide on his own when he was ready to move on to the next adventure. Reluctantly, I did just that. Using my technique of talking to his soul while his body slept, I told him that I would not interfere the next time he was presented with the choice. So far, thankfully, I guess he has decided to stay here.

I do believe we can interfere with a soul's choice to move on. Back in my Pentecostal days, I was in charge of a group of people who prayed over people and events affecting our community and our church. A beloved member of our church had suffered a stroke. We prayed and prayed and she eventually recovered. Then, a few months later, she died unexpectedly before we could pray the event away. It was then that I realized the power that we have to change the course of events. We have to be careful to always honor the free will of the person for whom we are praying. This lovely woman probably would have preferred to move on months before but we possibly prevented this by our prayers. She was forced to leave the earth quickly and unexpectedly to circumvent our interference.

Omens from Movies

Years ago, Spirit would give me omens from movies. At that time, I did not have the multitude of tools that I use today to receive guidance from the Spirit world, and movies were my escape from the world in which I lived. Movies told me I would be leaving the church, that my best friend would betray me but that eventually I would realize she had given me a gift, that I would leave my husband, and that I would fall in love again fairly quickly. Other than movies, I have been given omens in dreams, in unusual experiences in nature, in recurring cards from the tarot, recurring numbers, songs on the radio, and once even in a Chinese fortune cookie.

Omens from tarot cards

There is one particular card of the tarot which is, in itself, an omen. That card is the tower and the corresponding number is sixteen. I thought it only appropriate that this particular chapter be Chapter 16. In my previous chapter on the tarot I talked about how I once had a dream of the tower card and soon after that, our family was put through a very difficult experience.

I really can't explain why these things happen

Wouldn't it be better if we didn't know beforehand when a difficult experience was about to occur?

And why don't we receive warnings every time? Why do we sometimes get blindsided while other times we receive warnings for months before the event? I really don't have an answer. I guess as souls we have chosen to incarnate into an uncertain life. Part of the experience is the unknown. If we knew ahead of time when we were going to make a bad decision or have a challenge, maybe we would make different choices and avoid the learning experience.

Sometimes we get all the warning signs and we make bad decisions anyway. In hindsight, most of our really good learning experiences come from making bad decisions and fighting our way out of them. Do I get warnings or know ahead of time whenever clients or their family members are in danger? That is a really good question.

Predicting One's Demise

I do not do death predictions. Maybe some other mediums do, but I feel like our souls have decided beforehand to come into the earth realm. In my view, our soul knew it was going to be a challenge being here and gave us a variety of possible exit points. Depending on the choices we made while we were here, our soul gets to choose, or not choose, a possible exit point. If I, as a medium, see a possible exit point and let the cat out of the bag so to speak, then that person may choose to live their life differently than they would if they did not think they were going to pass. That being said, just because our souls know of the possible exit points does not mean our conscious minds know. Very few of us know when we are going to die. We may have feelings that we cannot explain, but our souls do not always tell us these things. There is also the possibility of a random occurrence that was not in the plan. I asked my Guides about this: "Does our soul always know? What if someone is just driving down the road and out of nowhere someone else collides with their car and immediately, they are whisked out of their body? Was that pre-planned?"

My Guides tell me that we sit down with our soul groups and our soul mentors and come up with a plan before incarnating. However, all plans are known to be changeable once we reach the earthly realm. When we get here, we voluntarily forget all about what has occurred before this lifetime. Since there are so many variables, such as the people who come and go from our lives and the choices those people make, it is impossible to predict with 100 percent accuracy exactly how our lives will play out.

It is like those improv comedy shows where a group of comedians are given a subject and they have to decide on the fly how to play it out in front of a live audience. As long as a soul's life plays out the way they have it planned, a psychic or a medium can read that person's energy and come up with a prediction based upon how the players are interacting with one another and the subject they have chosen. But if one person suddenly decides to quit the game or completely change the script, then the other actors in the play have to improvise and come up with a new plan. Any predictions that were made might have to be altered. Or perhaps the psychic saw ahead of time that one of the actors was going to quit the game. Would it be ethical to give that away?

Each specific reading and each specific client have to be taken on an individual basis. Maybe I will get a sign or a symbol that I don't realize is predicting a death. If I realize it, I might say I see a challenging scenario coming up soon. I will never say that I feel like someone is going to die, even if I think it. There was one time when I saw tulips and grass. I remember saying, "I am hearing someone talking about pushing tulips."

As soon as I said it, I realized the symbolism. Luckily, I guess the person who was talking had already passed and the client knew it.

Spirit also reminds me that if an event is set in stone and by some miraculous or supernatural knowing we are forewarned; we can do everything possible to prevent it but somehow that event still occurs. I am reminded of the tale of Sleeping Beauty. The child was placed under a curse that she would die before her sixteenth birthday. The king and queen did everything in their power to make sure that the event never occurred. Even though they were able to alter the curse and it ended up okay in the end, as the modern version of all fairy tales do, Sleeping Beauty did experience the events which were predicted.

In my thoughts at the present moment, there is fate and there is also free will.

Life is like the flowing of a river. There are huge rocks in the river that sometimes alter the flow of the river, but the rocks pretty much stay in the same place unless some huge event comes along to move them. The way the river flows may change, the course of an individual drop of water may be altered. But the river still flows and the rock still lies in the riverbed while the water flows over it and around it. On the other hand, if someone comes along and decides they are going to move that rock, then the water is going to flow somewhat differently because the placement of the rock has changed. Everything that was predicted to flow in a specific way has changed; not only the water and the banks of the river, but even the fish that perhaps laid their eggs under the rock. Should we then not move the rock? Who is to say?

I used to like to pray or ask my Guides for parking spaces close to the door when I was out shopping. My husband, always devil's advocate, remarked one day that in order for my guides to give me that parking spot, they had to take it away from someone else. What if the person from whom they whisked it away was disabled, or maybe their child was near death and they were hurrying into the store to pick up the prescription that would cure them? Should the Angels take that parking spot and give it to me just because I am lazy and don't feel like walking? Nowadays I tend not to ask for parking spaces unless it is pouring down rain or I am in a particular rush for some reason. On the other hand, I have noticed that sometimes the Guides will give me great parking spaces or even green lights without me having to ask! I tend to think of it as a kind of side benefit to really focusing on raising my vibration into a constant state of Divine Love and Peace. When I am walking around living my life in a higher vibration, it just seems like good things happen without me asking for it. When I am mad or depressed or not feeling well, I tend to attract red traffic lights and long lines at the grocery store.

We have to remember that every action in some way affects every other person, plant, and animal on the planet.

If we receive an omen of a pending troubling event, like a car accident, for example, and we change our normal behavior in order to avoid the disaster, how does that affect the flow of life?

Will we decide to take a different road home from work? If we do that, but the event was predestined to happen, will we cause that doom to shift to a different location? Perhaps the doom will still occur, but to someone else.

In the story of my husband and his near-death experience, I was forewarned several months ahead of its occurrence. I was having panic attacks about his death. I used the knowledge to speak to his soul and convince his soul to stay. That created within him a new perspective and appreciation for life. Several years later he became interested in investigating the paranormal. He unknowingly reignited within me a desire to use my gift of speaking to the invisible world of Spirit and over time, I have spoken to many, living and dead. If I had not been given that premonition, would our lives have played out in a different way? Or would some other event have occurred that would have brought us to the same end result? I guess these are questions for which we cannot possibly know the answer.

I have to believe that in some way I was destined to talk to the dead. If one path didn't lead me there, another one would have.

Omens are given to us for a reason.

I think Spirit wants us to get to where we will experience the life path we have chosen ahead of incarnation. Omens, just like dreams, messages from movies, tarot cards, or other divination techniques, are all meant to get us where we will experience the most joy from our chosen lives here in the earthly realm.

CHAPTER SEVENTEEN

SYNCHRONICITY

The dictionary defines synchronicity as the simultaneous occurrence of events which appear significantly related but have no discernible causal connection. Simply put, it's is when something happens at the same time as another event, that seems to tie everything together in a neat little bow. Synchronicity happens all the time. Most of the time we don't notice or we call it a coincidence.

The day my husband asked me out for dinner for what he affectionately calls our first non-date, I had eaten lunch at a Chinese restaurant. I loved fortune cookies despite the fact that the messages are usually pretty generic. That day my fortune cookie said, "Today you will meet the man of your dreams." Wait a minute. Fortune cookies are never that specific. Technically I had already met him, but that day I met him in a completely new way.

I find that at times in my life when I am about to enter a new chapter or alter my life path in some major way, I start hearing songs on the radio that talk about new beginnings. Or during difficult times the songs always seem to tell me, "Everything is going to be all right."

Just the other day I was driving in the car and actually sending some energy that was non-beneficial out of the experience of a client, at her request. Ha, yes, sometimes I do this while I am driving. When I was done, I happened to notice the words of the song on the radio saying, " I will go, go, go…"

Twice in my life I was approaching an upcoming move to a different house. Both times I had no intention of moving and really had no indication that a move was in my future. On both occasions, all the plants that lived in my home, which are many, outgrew their pots almost simultaneously. Intuitively I knew I was outgrowing my own pot and was about to be transplanted.

The Letter to Santa

In my working days, as part of my day job, I was tasked with answering letters that had been written to Santa. I happened to open one from a child who asked for two things—that his grandmother be healed of cancer, and the jacket from Michael Jackson's Thriller video. Two absolutely impossible tasks, right? I was so touched by the letter; I walked over to one of the supervisor's desks to show it to her. She was talking to another employee at that moment but she paused her conversation as I apologized for interrupting and told her about the letter. The interesting part of the story was about to occur.

The employee standing with us asked to look at the letter. When I showed it to him, he calmly exclaimed that the letter was from his grandson. His wife, unbeknownst to anyone, was in treatment for leukemia. He felt she was doing well and would probably recover, and acknowledged that his grandson had inherited a love for Michael Jackson from his mother.

That is synchronicity. I had not been in the habit of sharing children's letters. Normally I read them and replied with no fanfare. That day I decided to share and, not so coincidentally, the child's grandfather just happened to be in the same place at the same time.

Every day we can be a tool for the goodness of the Universe to bless others.

Once while working at the Post Office I was able to give a pen to a homeless girl down on her luck. It was just a pen. But to her it was a sign that the Universe was kind and things would get better. How did I know she had a thing for pens?

Synchronicity can also be a recurring series of numbers. Many people will report seeing repetitive numbers and I am no exception. Since I am fairly familiar with the art of numerology, I can receive messages from Spirit just by the numbers I see repetitively. Or perhaps I walk by a familiar object a hundred times and the 101st time I see a number that I hadn't before. When that happens, I know it is significant.

Our day to day lives are filled with synchronicity. We think about someone and they call, or we see something about them on the news or in the paper. We see a stranger who reminds us of a person we know and something significant happens to or about that person.

Many of the classes I have taken to hone my skills have been introduced to me in synchronistic ways. If I had not received a sign or a message beforehand, I would probably not have taken the class. Sometimes it is not the class that is important, but someone I meet while taking the class or someone with whom I engage in conversation with as a result of the class.

A lot of the clients that I see report finding me on websites I do not subscribe to, or finding me in an odd or out-of-the-ordinary way. I previously talked about a client or two who I unintentionally happened upon while performing my duties at my day job. What does this mean? My guides tell me there are several possibilities.

Because of the reality of collective consciousness, when a person puts out a request either consciously or unconsciously to their higher power, the souls that are receptive to being used as an answer to that request will be drawn to what is considered to be a chance meeting. The guides are really just collaborating to help the meeting actually take place. There is also the common universal principal of *like attracts like*. We are all just energetic magnets drawing to ourselves the experiences that we are ready to have and, just like magnets, other people that are in that same vibratory level will just naturally be drawn to an experience which will enhance the likelihood of a meeting.

Synchronicity then, is when two or more separate events come together in an unusual way and somehow seem to point to one another in some way.

A client came to me a year after her stepdaughter died asking for a sign of her presence. The same day her husband's phone rang and the number on the caller ID was the daughter's old number. When he picked up, the phone went dead. When he called it back, it was out of service. My ex-mother-in-law contacted me from the other side asking me to have my daughter contact her father, only to find out he had recently had a brush with death. My husband happened to think about an old schoolmate whom he had not seen in twenty years or more and a couple of days later he ran into him at a store.

Recently I was preparing to do a presentation via social media on the upcoming solstice and full moon. I wanted to share a couple of manifestation suggestions and I always like to know what sign the moon is in and what element is associated with that sign so that I can have some representation of that element in the ritual. I was kind of meditating, kind of thinking about the presentation, and the thought occurred to me that I needed to look up what sign the moon would be in on those days. *Gemini* quickly passed through my thoughts but I also felt like it would change before the next day. When I looked it up, I discovered the moon would be in Gemini on the solstice and transition into Cancer the next day for the full moon.

I could relate a hundred other events that could be considered synchronistic but I think you get the idea. Synchronicity reaffirms the knowledge that there is an Intelligence that we are all connected to that brings things together like a jigsaw puzzle when it is important to do so.

You could say that almost every reading or private session I do for a client is synchronistic in some way. Our people on the other side come together and give me a sign of their presence that is readily recognizable to the client. Even if the client isn't specifically asking to speak to their people, the information that comes through for them from their Angels, Spirit Guides, or the cards of the tarot, can be synchronistic. Spirit says something and it is exactly what someone needs to hear.

Eleven

Recently I was meditating before doing a phone session with a new client who had requested a soul healing. Spirit told me to be sure and access her soul at the age of eleven. A few minutes later she called. When I asked what happened to her at the age of eleven, she gasped. Her father died when she was eleven. A couple of months later she was molested by a relative who happened to be a priest. Later in the year her appendix burst. Obviously, her soul needed some healing from all of those events. Synchronicity.

Jesus and Reiki

I was teaching a Reiki class once and one of the students was a bit apprehensive. She had been brought up to be a Christian and had it in her mind that in some way Reiki was in conflict with her beliefs. When it came time to attune her to the energies of Reiki, I felt Jesus standing behind me. I felt His hands blend with my hands to transmit her attunement. Later when I shared with her what had happened, she admitted her concerns and was ecstatic to hear that her attunement came directly from Jesus! Of all the students I have worked with before and since, her session was the only one in which I sensed His specific presence during the process.

From these stories I hope you realize that the Universe is friendly and that there are a multitude of Benevolent Energies that collaborate to give you the experiences that you need to reinforce exactly what you need.

Those who are not in alignment energetically to the benevolence of the Universe will experience their lives in exactly the way they expect. If they believe the Universe to be unfriendly, they will experience exactly that. There will be synchronistic events in their lives that prove exactly what they believe. That is how the Universe works.

WHY ARE THEY TELLING ME THIS STUFF?

Every day is an adventure in possibility. We can wake up in the morning with the attitude of "Oh no, another day in hell," or we can awake with the song on our lips, "What adventure awaits me today?" Over time I am waking up less and less with a longing to be somewhere else or doing something else, and more with an attitude of gratitude for where I am, right here in this moment.

One day maybe the voices will stop talking to me and I will decide to be an artist or a bum on the beach. Or perhaps one day everyone will be able to converse with their people and animals on the other side, heal their own souls, receive their own guidance from their Guides, and my job will be eliminated. Right now, in this moment, they are speaking and I am doing my best to be a mouthpiece for Spirit. Every day I am learning and growing. As I get older, I am less worried about recognition and validation and more focused on contentment.

In days past, the messages came to me and I had no one to tell. I wrote them down. I told my small circle of friends. I remember having lunch with a friend one day and asking, "Why are they telling me this stuff? It has to be for something other than just my own information." I had visions of the messages being for the greater good and day after day I strived to shed the day job and give messages for a living. But my love of having a roof over my head and food in my belly kept me getting up every day and going to that job. As I trudged away performing my various duties, Spirit continued to speak to me.

Almost every day I received some sort of communication from someone or something with which people don't normally converse. Once when I was particularly discouraged, a blade of grass told me, "Keep growing. Every day I grow and grow. I reach for the sun. I have visions of grandeur. And once a week some big machine comes along and cuts me back down and I have to start all over again. I never give up or become despondent. I just pick myself up and keep growing." At that moment I realized it was not about growing tall and communicating some wise and all-knowing truth to those who were less connected than I. It was about being green and healthy and, along with all of the other blades of grass, being one small piece of life in a world where it was highly likely that there was something or someone bigger than myself that might come along and cut me back down to size.

As long as I wake every morning and bask in the beauty of the sunrise, thank the earth for giving me stability and a firm foundation on which to stand, I am okay. Every day, do what makes your heart sing. Know that no one can do what you do exactly the way you do it. Sing a song. Write a poem. Pick up trash. Be a light in a dark corner of the world. If you are shining your light and a rainstorm comes along and extinguishes the candle of your soul, reignite yourself and start again.

Life is all about the adventure. Sometimes we go through life and we never figure out what makes our hearts sing.

We don't realize that each moment is a miracle.

What makes my heart sing may be a burden for someone else. I love speaking with the dead and the voices in the Spirit world, but I have met many who spend their lives attempting to make the voices go away.

All I can say is, follow your joy. If you still have to get up in the morning and go to a job, then make sure you are the best hairdresser, trash collector, ditch digger, or CEO there is. No matter how important your job is, or how invisible, be the best at whatever you do. Find joy in your everyday tasks. Answer the phone, fix computers, teach children, change diapers, play football in the very best expression of your soul that you possibly can.

You never know what worlds are changed by the kind word you speak to a stranger, the pen you give to a homeless person, or the change you put in the parking meter for the next person to park. Shine. Grow. If you get mowed back down to size, then get up and grow some more.

Remember that the things you see and feel in the here and now are only a part of the total experience.

There are many rooms in the world of Spirit.

Just because you experience most of your life in a particular room, doesn't mean there isn't a whole world of adventures happening in the next room. Be open to other possibilities. If you begin having a nagging feeling that what you think about life and faith and belief and spirit is not the whole story, allow yourself to consider that there may be more. There are always *at least* two sides to every story.

If you don't believe me, I am sure you can find someone out there with a different version of the stories I present here.

Don't take my word for it, go out there and find out!

ABOUT THE AUTHOR

Joy Andreasen was born in a small town in Virginia to a middle-class Christian couple in the sixties. She spent the first thirty-five years of her life completely embracing the belief system she was born into. While attending a prophetic church in her town, she seemed to develop a knack for communicating messages from the Holy Spirit, a practice that was not only common but encouraged. Over time, however, her messages became increasingly at odds with the established belief system. After leaving her faith and subsequently her husband of eighteen years, she turned off the ability to communicate messages. After remarrying, her new husband developed an interest in the paranormal, and her gift was re-ignited. Maintaining her "day" job, she began developing and using her gift "on the side."

She finally retired after thirty-one years at the Post Office and began sharing her insights, messages, and energy healing abilities full time. She now teaches spiritually based classes, sees clients by phone, Zoom and in person, shares a message of the day on social media and occasionally chats via YouTube and Zoom She and her husband occasionally lecture at events on various paranormal subjects. This book is intended to familiarize readers with the different aspects of her work and contains thought provoking anecdotes and stories to back up her musings on the Spirit world.

REFERENCES

The following is a list of books, people, and online courses either alluded to in the text of this book or recommended as a continuation of your own personal spiritual quest.

Books

- Spirit Releasement Therapy: A Technique Manual, William A Baldwin, Headline Books, June 1995
- The Presence of the Soul, John L Payne, Findhorn Press June 2012
- The Way of the Shaman, Michael Harner, HarperOne, January 1990
- Soul Retrieval, Sandra Ingerman, HarperOne, Revised, August 2006
- Healing Ancestral Karma, Stephen A Farmer, Hierophant Publishing 2014

People

- Terri Rodabaugh, Medium trodes444@gmail.com
- Susan Lynne, Medium www.mediumlink.com
- Christen McCormack, www.ChristenMcCormack.com

Online Courses

- Christina Pratt, Healing with Your Well and Unwell Ancestors, the Shift Network
- Hank Wesselman, The Shamanic Path of Re-Enchantment, the Shift Network

No copyright information found for The Unquiet Grave by Anonymous and Henry Scott Holland's Death is Nothing At All

Made in the USA
Middletown, DE
25 October 2020

22724072R00099